YULE

Llewellyn's Sabbat Essentials

YULE

Rituals, Recipes & Lore for the Winter Solstice

Llewellyn Publications
Woodbury, Minnesota

FIRST EDITION
Eleventh Printing, 2021

Book design: Donna Burch-Brown
Cover art: iStockphoto.com/18232461/© Electric_Crayon
          iStockphoto.com/11042471/©Adyna
          Shutterstock/162597791/©Kovalevska
          Shutterstock/116499046/©Viktoria
Interior illustrations: Mickie Mueller

Llewellyn Publications is a registered trademark of Llewellyn Worldwide Ltd.

Library of Congress Cataloging-in-Publication Data
Pesznecker, Susan Moonwriter.
  Yule : rituals, recipes, and lore for the winter solstice / by Susan Pesznecker.
    pages cm. — (Llewellyn's sabbat essentials ; # 7)
  Includes bibliographical references and index.
  ISBN 978-0-7387-4451-3
1. Yule (Festival) I. Title.
  BF1572.Y85P47 2015
  394.261—dc23
                        2015015225

Llewellyn Publications
A Division of Llewellyn Worldwide Ltd.
2143 Wooddale Drive
Woodbury, MN 55125-2989
www.llewellyn.com

Printed in the United States of America

Contents

compassion, wisdom, insight, search for meaning, sacrifice, etc... ...tion and looking inward, evaluation, reflection, meditation, hiber... ...on and scrying, study, journaling, tool crafting, feasting, commu... ...work, deep ritual, vigil, personal retreat. Amaterasu, Baba ...a, Bruno, Cailleach, Carlin, Carravogue, Ceres, Demeter, ...olda, Kolmada, Lachesis, Marzena, Rind, Skadi, Snegu... Bacchus, Hodhr, Lugh, Saturn, Dilis Varsvlani, Cert, ...n Knight, Green Man, Holly King, Karkantzaros, Kne... ...itzelfrau, Pelznichol, Perchta, Samichlaus, Stallo, Ton... ...am, Egregores, green: evergreen, abundance, life, new beginnings ...wealth, gifts, prosperity, solar energy, red: holly berries and ... ...firce, fire, white: silence, calm peace, protecting, cardamom: d... ...ticism, psychic powers, cinnamon: access to astral and spirit... ...tuition strength, cloves: attraction, authority, healing power, ...th, intuition, renewal, transformation, vitality, mistletoe: peace, ...st, protection, nutmeg, alertness, awareness, inspiration, intelli... ...t: calm, divination, intuition, psychic powers, relaxation, rosem... ...anishing, divination, healing, mental clarity, physical and p... ...strength, sage: calm, concentration, confidence, health, and ...

LLEWELLYN'S SABBAT ESSENTIALS

LLEWELLYN'S SABBAT ESSENTIALS provides instruction and inspiration for honoring each of the modern witch's sabbats. Packed with spells, rituals, meditations, history, lore, invocations, divination, recipes, crafts, and more, each book in this eight-volume series explores both the old and new ways of celebrating the seasonal rites that act as cornerstones in the witch's year.

There are eight sabbats, or holidays, celebrated by Wiccans and many other Neopagans (modern Pagans) today. Together, these eight sacred days make up what's known as the Wheel of the Year, or the sabbat cycle, with each sabbat corresponding to an important turning point in nature's annual journey through the seasons.

Devoting our attention to the Wheel of the Year allows us to better attune ourselves to the energetic cycles of nature and listen to what each season is whispering (or shouting!) to us, rather than working against the natural tides. What better time to start new projects than as the earth reawakens after a long winter, and suddenly everything is blooming and growing and shooting up out of the ground again? And what better time to meditate and plan ahead than during the introspective slumber of winter? With Llewellyn's Sabbat Essentials, you'll learn how to focus on the spiritual aspects of the Wheel of the Year, how to move through it and with it in harmony, and how to celebrate your own ongoing growth and achievements. This may be your first book on Wicca, Witchcraft, or Paganism, or your newest addition to a bookcase or e-reader already crammed with magickal wisdom. In either case, we hope you will find something of value here to take with you on your journey.

Take a Trip Through the Wheel of the Year

The eight sabbats each mark an important point in nature's annual cycles. They are depicted as eight evenly spaced spokes on a wheel representing the year as a whole; the dates on which they fall are nearly evenly spaced on the calendar, as well.

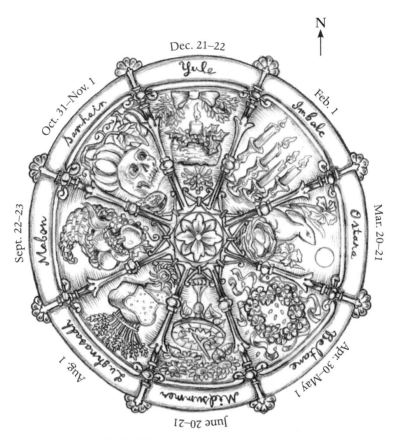

N

Dec. 21–22
Yule

Feb. 1
Imbolc

Oct. 31–Nov. 1
Samhain

Mar. 20–21
Ostara

Sept. 22–23
Mabon

Apr. 30–May 1
Beltane

Aug. 1
Lughnasad

Midsummer
June 20–21

Wheel of the Year—Northern Hemisphere
(All solstice and equinox dates are approximate,
and one should consult an almanac or a calendar
to find the correct dates each year.)

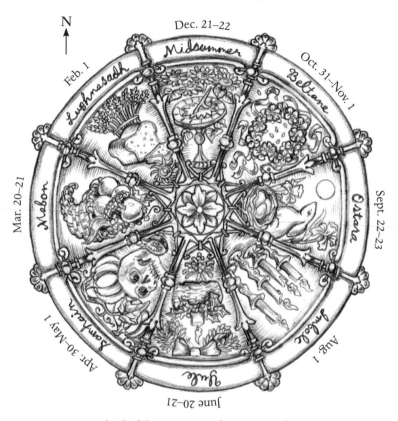

N

Dec. 21–22

Oct. 31–Nov. 1

Feb. 1

Lughnasadh

Midsummer

Beltane

Mar. 20–21

Mabon

Ostara

Sept. 22–23

Apr. 30–May 1

Samhain

Imbolc

Aug. 1

Yule

June 20–21

Wheel of the Year—Southern Hemisphere

The Wheel is comprised of two groups of four holidays each. There are four solar festivals relating to the sun's position in the sky, dividing the year into quarters: the Spring Equinox, the Summer Solstice, the Fall Equinox, and the Winter Solstice, all of which are dated astronomically and thus vary slightly from year to year. Falling in between these quarter days are the cross-quarter holidays, or fire festivals: Imbolc, Beltane, Lughnasadh, and Samhain. The quarters are sometimes called the Lesser Sabbats and the cross-quarters the Greater Sabbats, although neither cycle is "superior" to the other. In the Southern Hemisphere, seasons are opposite those in the north, and the sabbats are consequently celebrated at different times.

While the book you are holding only focuses on Yule, it can be helpful to know how it fits in with the cycle as a whole.

The Winter Solstice, also called Yule or Midwinter, occurs when nighttime has reached its maximum length; after the solstice, the length of the days will begin to increase. Though the cold darkness is upon us, there is a promise of brighter days to come. In Wiccan lore, this is the time when the young solar god is born. In some Neopagan traditions, this is when the Holly King is destined to lose the battle to his lighter aspect, the Oak King. Candles are lit, feasts are enjoyed, and evergreen foliage is brought in the house as a reminder that, despite the harshness of winter, light and life have endured.

At Imbolc (also spelled Imbolg), the ground is just starting to thaw, signaling that it's time to start preparing the fields for the approaching sowing season. We begin to awaken from our months of introspection and start to sort out what we have learned over that time, while also taking the first steps to make plans for our future. Some Wiccans also bless candles at Imbolc, another symbolic way of coaxing along the now perceptibly stronger light.

On the Spring Equinox, also known as Ostara, night and day are again equal in length, and following this, the days will grow longer than the nights. The Spring Equinox is a time of renewal, a time to plant seeds as the earth once again comes to life. We decorate eggs as a symbol of hope, life, and fertility, and we perform rituals to energize ourselves so that we can find the power and passion to live and grow.

In agricultural societies, Beltane marked the start of the summer season. Livestock were led out to graze in abundant pastures and trees burst into beautiful and fragrant blossom. Rituals were performed to protect crops, livestock, and people. Fires were lit and offerings were made in the hopes of gaining divine protection. In Wiccan mythos, the young god impregnates the young goddess. We all have something we want to harvest by the end of the year—plans we are determined to realize—and Beltane is a great time to enthusiastically get that process in full swing.

The Summer Solstice is the longest day of the year. It's also called Litha, or Midsummer. Solar energies are at their apex, and the power of nature is at its height. In Wiccan lore, it's the time when the solar god's power is at its greatest (so, paradoxically, his power must now start to decrease), having impregnated the maiden goddess, who then transforms into the earth mother.

In some Neopagan traditions, this is when the Holly King once again battles his lighter aspect, this time vanquishing the Oak King. It's generally a time of great merriment and celebration.

At Lughnasadh, the major harvest of the summer has ripened. Celebrations are held, games are played, gratitude is expressed, and feasts are enjoyed. Also known as Lammas, this is the time we celebrate the first harvest—whether that means the first of our garden crops or the first of our plans that have come to fruition. To celebrate the grain harvest, bread is often baked on this day.

The Autumn Equinox, also called Mabon, marks another important seasonal change and a second harvest. The sun shines equally on both hemispheres, and the lengths of night and day are equal. After this point, the nights will again be longer than the days. In connection with the harvest, the day is celebrated as a festival of sacrifice and of the dying god, and tribute is paid to the sun and the fertile earth.

To the Celtic people, Samhain marked the start of the winter season. It was the time when the livestock was slaughtered and the final harvest was gathered before the inevitable plunge into the depths of winter's darkness. Fires were lit to help wandering spirits on their way, and offerings were given in the names of the gods and the ancestors. Seen as a beginning, Samhain is now often called the Witches' New Year. We honor our ancestors, wind down our activities, and get ready for the months of introspection ahead ... and the cycle continues.

The Modern Pagan's Relationship to the Wheel

Modern Pagans take inspiration from many pre-Christian spiritual traditions, exemplified by the Wheel of the Year. The cycle of eight festivals we recognize throughout modern Pagandom today was never celebrated in full by any one particular pre-Christian culture. In the 1940s and 1950s, a British man named Gerald Gardner created the new religion of Wicca by drawing on a variety of cultures and traditions, deriving and adapting practices from pre-Christian religion, animistic beliefs, folk magick, and various shamanic disciplines and esoteric orders. He combined multicultural equinox and solstice traditions with Celtic feast days and early European agricultural and pastoral celebrations to create a single model that became the framework for the Wiccan ritual year.

This Wiccan ritual year is popularly followed by Wiccans and witches, as well as many eclectic Pagans of various stripes. Some Pagans only observe half of the sabbats, either the quarters or the cross-quarters. Other Pagans reject the Wheel of the Year altogether and follow a festival calendar based on the culture of whatever specific path they follow rather than a nature-based agrarian cycle. We all have such unique paths in Paganism that it is important not to make any assumptions about another's based on your own; maintaining an open and positive attitude is what makes the Pagan community thrive.

Many Pagans localize the Wheel of the Year to their own environment. Wicca has grown to become a truly global religion, but few of us live in a climate mirroring Wicca's British Isles origins. While traditionally Imbolc is the beginning of the thaw and the awakening of the earth, it is the height of winter in many northern climes. While Lammas may be a grateful celebration of the harvest for some, in areas prone to drought and forest fires it is a dangerous and uncertain time of year.

There are also the two hemispheres to consider. While it's winter in the Northern Hemisphere, it's summer in the Southern Hemisphere. While Pagans in America are celebrating Yule and the Winter Solstice, Pagans in Australia are celebrating Midsummer. The practitioner's own lived experiences are more important than any dogma written in a book when it comes to observing the sabbats.

In that spirit, you may wish to delay or move up celebrations so that the seasonal correspondences better fit your own locale, or you may emphasize different themes for each sabbat as you experience it. This series should make such options easily accessible to you.

No matter what kind of place you live on the globe, be it urban, rural, or suburban, you can adapt sabbat traditions and practices to suit your own life and environment. Nature is all around us; no matter how hard we humans try to insulate ourselves from nature's cycles, these recurring seasonal changes are inescapable. Instead of swimming against the tide, many modern Pagans embrace each season's unique energies, whether dark, light, or in between, and integrate these energies into aspects of our own everyday lives.

Llewellyn's Sabbat Essentials series offers all the information you need in order to do just that. Each book will resemble the one you hold in your hands. The first chapter, *Old Ways*, shares the history and lore that have been passed down, from mythology and pre-Christian traditions to any vestiges still seen in modern life. *New Ways* then spins those themes and elements into the manners in which modern Pagans observe and celebrate the sabbat. The next chapter focuses on *Spells and Divination* appropriate to the season or based in folklore, while the following one, *Recipes and Crafts*, offers ideas for decorating your home, hands-on crafts, and recipes that take advantage of seasonal offerings. The chapter *Prayers and Invocations* provides ready-made calls and prayers you may use in ritual, meditation, or journaling. The *Rituals of Celebration* chapter provides three complete rituals: one for a solitary, one for two people, and one for a whole group such as a coven, circle, or grove. (Feel free to adapt each or any ritual to your own needs, substituting your own offerings, calls, invocations, magickal workings, and so on. When planning a group ritual, try to be conscious of any special needs participants may have. There are many wonderful books available that delve into the fine points of facilitating ritual if you don't have experience in this department.) Finally, in the back of the book you'll find a complete list of correspondences for the holiday, from magickal themes to deities to foods, colors, symbols, and more.

By the end of this book you'll have the knowledge and the inspiration to celebrate the sabbat with gusto. By honoring the Wheel of the Year, we reaffirm our connection to nature so that as her endless cycles turn, we're able to go with the flow and enjoy the ride.

OLD WAYS

compassion, resistance, insight, search for meaning, sacrifice, etc...

...on and looking inward, evaluation, reflection, meditation, hiber...

...n and scrying, study, journaling, tool crafting, feasting, commu...

...work, deep ritual, vigil personal retreat. Amaterasu, Baba...

..., Bruno, Cailleach, Carlin, Carravogue, Ceres, Demeter, D...

...lda Koliada, Lachesis, Marzana, Rind Skadi, Snegur...

...Bacchus, Wodin, Lugh, Saturn, Dilis Varsslави, Cert, E...

...Knight, Green Man, Holly King, Karkantzaros, Knec...

...utzelfrau, Pelznichol, Perchta, Samichlaus, Stella, Tom...

...nn, Egregores, green: evergreen, abundance, life, new beginnings,

...wealth, gifts, prosperity, solar energy, red: holly berries and p...

...ica, fire, white: silence, calm peace, protecting, cardamom: di...

...tasм, psychic powers, cinnamon: access to astral and spiritua...

...tion strength, cloves: attraction, authority, healing power, pr...

...t, intuition, renewal, transformation, vitality, mistletoe: peace,

...t, protection, nutmeg, alertness, awareness, inspiration, intelli...

...t calm, divination, intuition, psychic powers, relaxation, rosema...

...anishing, divination, healing, mental clarity, physical and ps...

...strength, sage: calm concentration, confidence, health and...

*T*HERE'S SOMETHING ABOUT this time of year, something about winter and Yule that pulls deep at my heartstrings, making me want to celebrate out loud one moment and retreat to a quiet corner the next. To me, this is a most magickal time of year; it's the time when Mother Earth goes quiet, yet if we listen really carefully, we can still hear her heart beating. It's a profound and important time to curl up and engage in the solitary act of contemplation as we embrace what should be a natural time of sleep. It's also time to honor the real and spiritual "dark" and to rejoice in the return of the light, celebrating and passing traditions with friends and family.

These feelings go all the way back to our ancestors, the ancients, who lived their lives according to the constantly shifting rhythms of the great seasonal Wheel. In the spring, they planted crops, harvesting them through the summer and fall. As fall progressed, they "wintered in"—storing food, gathering fuel for winter fires, and putting their fields to bed. When winter came, the people took to their dwellings and passed the cold, dark months living off of their stored bounty, telling stories around the fire, making risky hunting forays for scarce winter meat, and hoping that they had prepared enough food and firewood to last until spring. Going to bed early helped conserve candles, oils, and other light sources, and rising late—staying snug in their beds—helped save heating fuel. Their food-stuffs changed with the winter season, too, focusing on gourds and other vegetables, grains, and meats that could be preserved or stored. In a very real way, they hibernated—their daily rhythms quieting and falling in sync with the sleeping world around them.

Today, many of us have forgotten how to "hibernate" successfully. We maintain the same routines year-round, and people often grumble about the winter months instead of embracing winter's place in the great seasonal Wheel. In our modern world, we can maintain a consistent temperature in our homes year round, a flip of a switch providing summer-bright lighting late into the winter's night. Our diet need not change either. We can eat raspberries and spring greens year round, if we're willing to pay for them. These actions threaten to pull us desperately out of sync with winter's rhythms, and this may cause problems. In fact, one of the newest theories regarding seasonal affective disorder links it to fighting against winter's rhythms instead of embracing them. As modern Pagans, it can be difficult to embrace Midwinter when we're so disconnected from ancient agricultural cycles—we'll explore this more in the next chapter.

But have no fear, for the celebrations of winter persist, and they serve an important function in reminding everyone that the Wheel keeps on turning. They connect us to the essential "feel" of winter, and particularly during the month of December—the time of the Winter Solstice, often referred to as Yule—people are moved to come together with family and friends to feast and celebrate, to embrace the very soul of the season. In this book, we'll explore those motivations as well as a treasure trove of ideas for truly celebrating the Winter Solstice. And Midwinter deserves our enthusiasm, for it's a truly wonderful time of year and one of astounding magickal importance.

Winter Solstice, Midwinter, and Yule: The Lexicon

Winter Solstice is a term describing a specific astronomical alignment, which we'll get to in just a bit. *Solstice* means "sun stands still," referring to the sun's low, slow, almost imperceptible movement at solstice time. As for "Midwinter," it's used as a synonym for the Winter Solstice. Yule, on the other hand, is typically linked to a number of religious celebrations and spiritual traditions.

According to the *Oxford English Dictionary (OED)*—the definitive dictionary of the modern English language—*Yule* descends from the Old English *geól*, and may refer to (1) Christmas day or Christmastide; (2) the Old Norse *jól*, meaning a heathen feast lasting twelve days (with possible links to Odin and the Wild Hunt); (3) the Old Anglian *giuli*, recorded by Bede in 726 CE, referring to the name of December and January; (4) the Old Norse *ýlir*, the month beginning on the second day of the week falling within November 10–17; and (5) the Gothic *jiuleis* in *fruma jiuleis*, meaning "November." There may also be a Germanic variant of "Yule" (*jeul-*, *jegul-*, and **je ul)*, but this remains obscure. There is also a suggestion of the word's use in Norse poetry as a synonym for "feast."

The *OED* also tells us that the word "Yule" has been widely used since the mid-1800s as an informal term for Christmas and the related festivities, while "Good Yule" has come to be an expression of joy or excitement in terms of Midwinter celebrations. The *OED* suggests the word *Yule* may be a sound variation of the word "wheel," whether in terms of the turning of the seasons, the circular motion of the sun, or the wheels of Odin's chariot. In casual use, some believe that the word may be related to expressions of "joy" or "jolly."

The ancient Romans had their own words for Yule time, too: *Dies Natalis Solis Invicti*—the birthday of the unconquerable sun. At one time the Romans celebrated this time of year as the birth of their beloved Mithras, a solar god, closely linking this event with the solstice and the return of light. Around the fourth century, the Church of Rome began substituting the "birth of the son" with "the birth of the *Son*," intuiting the Christian Jesus as the one who would bring light and life to the world. Note that modern theologians agree that Jesus, regardless of the details of his life, was likely born during the springtime; however, Midwinter was settled on as the time to honor his birth date as the Pagan people were already used to celebrating the return of light to the world, their lives being metaphorically reborn with each Winter Solstice.

Does all of this help us understand what Yule means? Yes and no. While the meaning of the term may not be crystal clear, it's easy to see that the word has been in use for many centuries across a broad range of civilizations and traditions. It has a rich history.

What about December?

The word *December* actually means "ten" or "tenth." As if the cup of inspiration ran dry following the creative and oft-inspired deity-naming of the months January through August, the remaining months were simply assigned numbers. The name "September" actually means "seven." It may seem that it should mean "nine," since the modern calendar counts it as the ninth month), but the original calendar had two fewer months than the present Roman version. Thus, *September* means "seven," *October* means "eight," *November* means "nine," and *December* is named for the tenth month in the original Roman calendar.

Eventually the Romans added January and February to the calendar, thus making December the twelfth month, but they left it with its original name to avoid confusion.

Some sources believe December may also reference the goddess Decima, considered by many to be the Roman equivalent of the Greek Lachesis. Both goddesses were believed to have the job of measuring out the life thread of mortals and had the ability to decide a mortal's lot in life and how long the mortal would live. As the middle member of the *Parcae,* or Three Fates, Decima is often thought to be the personification of the present, possibly referencing the real-time death/rebirth nature of the Winter Solstice (Armour). Her ability to "spin death" may also be a neat allusion to the metaphorical silence and symbolic death of Midwinter, the quiet that must precede renewal.

December is also called "Holy Month" or *heilagmanoth* by the Franks, *Aerra Geola*, "The Month Before Yule" by the Anglo-Saxons, and *Mi na Nollag*, or "Christmas month," by the Irish. Each of these names clearly speaks to the winter festival traditions that abound at this time of year.

The Astronomical Cycle of Yule

Midwinter is also clearly linked to astronomy and the movements of the heavens. At the Winter Solstice, the great seasonal Wheel reaches a turning point and begins to rotate back toward the light. With the passing of the Winter Solstice, the days lengthen and the temperature slowly rises. It's not surprising that ancient peoples rejoiced at Yule, for with the arrival of the solstice they knew that winter's challenges would soon ebb and warmth, light, and abundant food would return.

The astronomical Winter Solstice—the longest night of the year—usually falls on December 21 or 22. The Winter Solstice is part of an astronomical cycle that recurs each year with only slight variation. For those in the Northern Hemisphere, the Winter Solstice marks the beginning of winter—the shortest day and longest night of the year—and the farther north one moves, the more profound the effects. Those living on the forty-fifth parallel, halfway between the equator and the North Pole, will experience about eight and a half hours of light and fifteen and a half hours of darkness at the solstice. Go farther north to Anchorage, Alaska, and the Winter Solstice sun rises at about ten a.m. and goes down by three p.m., after only clearing a few degrees above the horizon. For people within the Arctic Circle, the Winter Solstice means near complete darkness, and at the North Pole, the sun doesn't rise at all.

What creates Midwinter's longest night? Everyone knows that Earth rotates around the sun, but Earth isn't "straight up and down" in its rotation: it's actually tilted 23.5 degrees off-axis. Since Earth is tilted, different parts of the globe are closer to or farther away from the sun at different times of the year.

This is what creates the year's four seasons: spring, summer, autumn, and winter. When the part of Earth one resides on is tilted more toward the sun, that hemisphere experiences a warmer season (spring or summer), while the hemisphere on the other side and tilted away from the sun experiences the opposite colder season (fall or winter). The closer one lives to the equator, the less axial tilt is present and the less variation there is between summer and winter; conversely, the closer one lives to the North or South Pole, the more extreme the seasonal variation.

Another key aspect of the Winter Solstice is that the sun doesn't appear to rise very high in the sky, typically reaching a point only about twenty degrees (or even less) above the horizon. This is much lower than the Midsummer sun, which appears to peak almost directly overhead. Because of its shallow arc, the Winter Solstice sun appears to move slowly and even seems to pause and become motionless at its highest point. And indeed, the word *solstice* is derived from two Latin words: *sol* meaning "sun," and *sistere*, "to cause to stand still," (i.e., "sun stands still"). Because the winter sun's rays strike Earth at a shallow angle, they generate little warmth, resulting in the cooler temperatures most associate with winter. That said, the Winter Solstice transitions into the astrological sun sign period of Capricorn—an earth sign and an excellent connection between the Midwinter season and the sleeping (but soon to awaken) land.

To identify the precise time for Yule in astronomical terms, consult a Farmer's Almanac or look online—one of the wonderful aspects of the Web is the ability to answer these kinds of questions in an instant, regardless of one's location or time zone.

The Mythological Cycles of Yule

Each of the Pagan Old Way traditions associates Yule with a specific mythological cycle, either pertaining to deity figures (gods, goddesses, holy infants), to winter's dangerous ferocity, or to the return and renewal of light and life. In folkloric terms, a "myth" is a story that a culture holds sacred in terms of its origins, and a myth is one that is regarded as important and retold from one generation to the next. Myths and stories of Midwinter appear throughout the world's cultural and religious traditions and are interwoven with folklore and legend. Let's examine several.

The Goddesses, Queens, Mothers, and Heroines

Winter is definitely a mother-centric time, for it is women who nurture life's sparks within their bodies and give birth to that life in its realized form. In addition to stories of birth, many women of legend are tagged with measuring out life or even bringing it to an end. Throughout world cultures past and present, winter myth and legend abound with reverent stories of these powerful female figures.

In Norwegian tradition, Frigg (or Frigga) is counted as the goddess of winter, and is strongly associated with the Winter Solstice (Lindow). The Solstice is known in Northern Europe as "the Mother Night," for it is on this night that Frigg labored to birth the sun into the world. Even today, many Norse women invoke Frigg's name for a healthy pregnancy.

Holda (also Frau Holle or Hulda, "kindly one") is the Germanic goddess of Christmas and the bringer of both prosperity and fertility—which were closely related in past cultures, where a large family helped ensure a successful life. Another Germanic tradition holds that a forest goddess shape-shifts into a white doe and goes into a sacred cave in order to give birth to the sun of the New Year. This happens on "Mothers' Night."

The Saxons used the term *Modranicht* (also *Mōdraniht*), "Night of the Mothers" or "Mother's Night," to describe the dark nights of this time of year. According to Bede's translations, Mother's Night was originally a Pagan Midwinter celebration, but the Saxons later shifted the celebration to Christmas Eve, and included an animal sacrifice to appease winter's angry gods (Wallis). The event may also be linked to the Germanic *Matron* cult, whose Mōdraniht sacrificial festival was held for the *Matres* and *Matrons*, German female deities. At least one source suggests that Modranicht may have originally taken place on Samhain as a festival of the dead, after which it was later moved to Yule (Sacred Texts).

Winter's female deities were often linked to the season's fierceness as well. In Celtic theology, the Mother is the "old one," also known as Cailleach, the divine hag-crone who rules the year's winter half between Samhain (October 31) and Bealltainne (May 1) and brings the icy cold death and darkness of winter and wildness to the world (McNeill, 119). Skadi (also Skathi or Skadl) is the Scandinavian goddess of winter. Able to control the winter weather, she is said to reside high in the snowy mountains and loves to ski throughout her domain, scattering snowstorms behind her.

The Greek goddess Alcyone, taking the form of a kingfisher, takes to her nest every winter for two weeks, and during this time, the seas are said to be calm (Smith, 108). In a variation of this Greek legend, a grieving wife named Alcyone throws herself into the sea upon discovering the drowned body of her beloved husband, Ceyx. The gods take pity on the pair, transforming them into kingfishers with the power to still the stormy seas for fourteen days around the time of the Winter Solstice— seven days before and seven after—while they build their nest and hatch their young. The so-called Halcyon Days have thus come to represent a time of peaceful quiet, happiness, and good weather around the time of Midwinter.

Other goddess forms often linked to Midwinter include Bona Dea (a Roman women's goddess of abundance and prophecy; she was associated with a winter festival that involved ritual house cleansing and an all-female ritual of bounty and fertility), St. Lucy (a Roman/Greek woman who became a Christian martyr for uncertain reasons; she is celebrated on December 13, and in keeping with Midwinter, her festival is considered a celebration of light), and Befana (an Italian witch-crone who gives gifts to children on January 5; she may be linked to the Roman New Year goddess Strenua or to the Russian legend of Babushka).

The Gods, Kings, Fathers, and Heroes

Where the women of winter are typically credited with the struggles of birth and death, the male figures are invariably shown as heroes, battling against adversity or to achieve a needed foothold and ensure life continues as it should. Traditions of a "winter king" around the Winter Solstice go back to ancient celebrations of the sun's rebirth. Winter's male deity figures frequently symbolize or represent the sun, ideals of generative male fertility, and the return of light and vigor to the world.

The early Etruscans and Romans viewed the sun as a male deity and celebrated the "Birth of the Unconquered Sun" around solstice time. In 10 BCE, the Roman emperor Augustus installed Apollo as the reigning "version" of the solar god, and celebratory games and feasting were held in Apollo's honor. Lugh, an Irish mythological/deity figure often displayed with solar imagery and linked to solar celebrations, is likened by many to the Greek god Apollo, whose golden chariot drove the sun across the sky. However, the mythological cycle associated with Lugh shows no explicit connection between him and the Winter Solstice.

Apollo's popular importance was eventually superseded by the Persian deity Mithras and the subsequent Roman cult of Mithraism. Interestingly, Mithras's story is not well recorded in ancient sources; the information we have about him is mostly from secondary legends and depictions on monuments. He appears in the record between 1 and 4 CE as a figure who was born from a rock. His followers were all male, and his temples were always pictured as being underground. In those temples, he is depicted as slaying a bull, after which he greets the sun, who bows down to him in reverence. Based on these depictions, he has long been considered a Roman solar deity and is described as *sol invictus* (the unconquered son) in inscriptions.

As mentioned earlier, Mithras's December 25 birthday has led many to imagine a supposed connection between his and Jesus's birth, and this belief has persisted—despite the fact that there is no true connection. Indeed, there is no actual evidence that Mithras was born on December 25, and scholars agree that there is no actual relationship between Christianity and the cult of Mithraism.

Another connection to the winter god figures is the Roman festival of Saturnalia, held in honor of the agricultural god Saturn and celebrated between December 17–23 (Matthews, 23). The ancient Saturnalia was a time of feasting and merriment at the end of the harvesting and wine-making seasons. Presents were exchanged, sacrifices offered, and masters turned tables and served their slaves, all in Saturn's name—a celebration of the male generative force.

The ancient festival took place in the Roman temple of Saturn; today's modern Pagans keep the festival alive in homes, halls, and fields. Near the end of the fourth century, Saturnalia was moved to the New Year and more or less merged with the Kalends of January, a Roman Midwinter celebration. A number of Midwinter festivals worldwide would spring from the Kalends, including the *Calends* of Provence, France; Poland's *Kolenda;* the Czech Republic's *Koleda*; Russia's *Kolada*; Lithuania's *Koledos*; and in Wales and Scotland, *Calenig* and *Calluin* (Matthews, 24).

Traditions of winter kingship persisted into the Middle Ages with stories of the "Green King of Winter" and his symbolic quest to win the hand of the Spring Maiden. The image of the Green King surfaces over and over again in the myths of King Arthur, Gawain, "Robin in the Green," and the archetypical Green Man—tropes echoed today in poetry, carols, mummering (a traditional work of drama), and even in the legends of the modern Santa Claus and the New Year's Father Time.

In *The Winter Solstice*, John Matthews explores an interesting take on the solar god, writing about the "Green Guest." Matthews describes the Green Knight, an Arthurian figure who came to King Arthur's hall as the Christmas festivities were getting under way, offering a strange game—that someone should strike him with his great axe, on the understanding that he will return the blow in a year's time.

> Only Gawain is brave enough to accept the challenge, and he undergoes many trials before the tale ends. For once his head has been severed, the Green Knight is able to pick it up, and await the coming of the challenger—a trick that Gawain is not able to do. The story is a wonderful one, and ancient. The Green Knight is the incarnate spirit of Winter, able to present his frightening challenge as the prelude to a battle for the hand of the Spring Maiden. (Matthews, 8)

Matthews sees this story as emblematic of Midwinter, hinting at the dark ferocity and the essential nature of this time of year, at the idea of battling back the wild darkness to make way for rebirth and renewal: the return of the light.

Revivalist Celtic traditions identify Midwinter as the time when the Oak King wins the battle against the Holly King, a battle that will reverse stakes at Midsummer. These ideas, inspired by Sir James George Frazer's *The Golden Bough*, focus on the dualistic battle between the forces of light and dark, characterizing it as a cycle that must be maintained in order for life to continue.

Yule's Fools and Misrules

In times past, many Midwinter celebrations featured dancing, feasting, and merrymaking, most of which weren't anywhere near the Church's idea of proper decorum at that time. Collectively, the uproarious events that popped up around the solstice were often called "Feasts of Fools." These were likely attempts by the people to escape the iron-fisted rule of the Church. In England, a "lord of misrule" was eventually appointed from the local lords and nobles and entrusted with watching over the festivities to make sure they didn't get too far out of hand. These events—also known as "misrules"—included everything from wild parties to over-the-top feasts to mock religious ceremonies, always with an air of sacrilege, satire, and barely controlled chaos.

Saturnalia would fit into the "misrules" category, ruled over by a spontaneously selected "mock king" whose task was to look and behave as foolishly as possible. In addition, slaves and masters (or in today's times, bosses and their underlings) traded places for the duration of the festival. While the point was serious—to ensure that crops would grow again when the sun and warmth arrived—the actual festivities were loud and ribald.

Despite efforts by the Church to quell these events (which sound a lot like today's Mardi Gras festivities), the Feast of Fools persisted in parts of Europe well into the seventeenth century. The idea of fools and misrules carried on into the traditions of mummers and Morris dancers and also to the celebration known as "the Twelve Days of Christmas," which commences on Christmas Day and extends through January 5. Such events were the people's way of embracing recurring symbols and celebrations and bringing light into the dark depths of Midwinter. These ideas haven't changed much: many people today still frame the holiday season with a series of parties and get-togethers with friends and family, a way of bringing a little misrule into a quiet, dark corner of the year.

Coming on the heels of the fools and misrules are the mummers and Morris dancers, where different cultures act out the season of Midwinter using drama and dance to form regional customs and traditions. Matthews tells us that in Britain, "mummer plays" are still performed today throughout solsticetide, providing a reenactment of the ritual slaying of the dark winter and rebirth of the coming light (Matthews, 33).

The Morris dance consists of a number of dancers—usually men—who carry out complex, unison dances while wearing outlandish costumes and carrying sticks. Traditionally, the dancers are unmasked but wear bowler-style hats. They may dance through the streets, but they often go door-to-door begging for libations as a reward for their entertainment. Mummers and Morris dancer traditions continue to this day in many places and have spawned a number of winter traditions. Modern Philadelphia has a notable mummer's procession on New Year's Day. According to Matthews, "The procession is so large that it takes most of the day to pass by City Hall, and includes every imaginable kind of costumed performer."

Another aspect of mummering and Morrising is the presence of the "Jolly Old 'Oss," the hobbyhorse. The hobby- or stick horse is common in old Pagan celebrations and often appears in Beltane revelries and pops up in many mummer plays or Morris dances. The horse is thought to be a reference to ancient shamanistic practices, with shamans providing intercession between humans and gods, perhaps providing a key appeal for the sun's return (Matthews, 34).

Gift Giving

Gift giving has long been a tradition during Midwinter. Some of the earliest gifts were offerings to placate the winter gods and goddesses and ask for their intercession to prevent famine, stop freezing weather, etc. Other gifts were given as entreaties—hoping to gain the gods' favor and benefit from it. This approach applied to the wee folk's favor, too: take, for instance, the Swedish *Tomte*, a kind of Sweden-specific gnome. The Tomte live in and around Swedish houses, barns, and sheds. They're said to be mostly benevolent creatures, and as long as they're shown the proper respect—including leaving small gifts spontaneously and during the cold winter—they will protect the home from accidents and disasters. It is said that the *Tomte* particularly appreciate bowls of porridge.

Midwinter gifts could represent a reward or incentive for good performance or behavior. For example, consider St. Nicholas Day, celebrated on December 6 throughout many European countries. Children who are well-behaved and obedient will find that St. Nicholas fills their stockings or shoes with candy and gifts, while those who've been naughty may only find twigs, coal, and small stones.

Gifts in the forms of charms, talismans, or the like were given to offset danger or ensure safe travel. Others were given as an homage, e.g., giving abundantly to one's landowner or patron. For example, it was customary for the Romans to make gifts called *strenae* at the New Year. The word *strenae* is connected with the name of a Sabine tutelary goddess, Strenia, who corresponds to the Roman Salus, and from whose precinct beside the *Via Sacra* at Rome consecrated branches were carried up to the Capitoline at the New Year (UPenn). The strenae consisted of bay and palm branches, honeyed sweetmeat, and figs or dates. Gilded fruits, pieces of money (especially those stamped with a Janus head—a reference to the god who could see into the past, present, and future), and small bronze or terra cotta lamps were also given at this time, particularly to one's patrons, emperors, or other officials.

And of course, other gifts were given as gestures of love or good will. Gifts could be given in the form of service, too. Most people today find this kind of giving to be the greatest joy of our modern season.

The Yule Log

In olden times, the Yule log was traditionally made of oak, although a log of ash was said to bring luck and insight. The first step in preparing for the Yule log ceremony was the cleansing and blessing of the home. The women of the hearth would do this cleansing, while the oldest or "senior" male of the household searched for just the right log. The largest possible log was selected, and it might take several family members to drag a really big Yule log home, after which it was trimmed to fit into the fireplace. Decorative carvings were added next, often resembling the shape of a Cailleach—the Celtic mother crone. As the embodiment of cold and death, she was tossed into the fire so that the family could watch as "winter" was replaced by heat and light, a ritual in keeping with the burning log's representation of the waxing solar year, Winter Solstice to Summer Solstice.

The carved log was festooned with greenery and anointed with ale, mead, or whiskey. The log was lit on solstice eve, ideally on the first try and using a piece of the previous year's log as kindling. Once lit, it was watched over through the night, with wishes and toasts made over the log and stories told in its presence. If the Yule log burned on until morning, it was considered a most positive omen.

If you have a fireplace, you can embrace the ritual of the Yule log. You might be lucky enough to have a Yule log stashed away from last year. If not, make your own from a sturdy piece of well-seasoned firewood or a piece of dry "found wood." (It's considered very bad luck to cut a Yule log from a living tree!) Even a sturdy branch can symbolize the Yule log if needed.

Before lighting, prepare your log in sacred fashion. Anoint the wood with pine, cedar, juniper, or other evergreen oils, concentrating on a "good Yule" and giving thanks for the ways the evergreens endure and the way the wood helps protect us from the cold. A pocket knife or wood burner can be used to carve runic signs, writing, or sigils into the wood as a way of making offerings to the Yule fire, or use ink pens to write on the wood's surface. Written prayers and petitions can be tied to the log with Yule-colored ribbons or cotton string. Work with correspondences of the Yule log: endurance, strength, triumph, protection, and luck.

Light your Yule log with ceremony, ideally in a dark room. For a magickal special effect, light it with a no-match technique such as flint-and-steel or with concealed fire starters impregnated with beeswax and essential oils. Contemplate the miracle of fire—warmth and light—and the mystery of the fire's emergence from the log. As the smoke rises, imagine your prayers, petitions, and wishes being sent to the guardians and shining ones in the smoke. You may wish to engage in a little fire scrying as you stare into the flames. If your ceremony involves others, be sure to offer cheers and toasts and tell good stories as you watch your log.

When taking down this year's solstice tree, cut off a portion of the trunk to serve as next year's Yule log. Rub it with this year's log's ashes, label it clearly (so no one mistakes it for ordinary wood), and put it away until next year.

The New Year

The modern Gregorian calendar (GC) marks January 1 as the start of a new year, and today's calendar years follow this pattern. This was not always the case, though.

An early predecessor of our modern calendar was the Roman calendar (RC), which was in place from the founding of Rome to the dissolution of the Roman Empire in 476 CE. Several versions of the RC were created, making adjustments to the number and length of months and to various cycles of days. In the earliest RCs, the New Year was based on the "consular year" and was linked to the dates when Roman consuls took office: at different times, this varied from May 1 to March 15 and finally, after the months of *Januarius* and *Februarius* were added, to January 1 (Bennet). Experts are uncertain as to exactly when January 1 was made the definitive New Year, but they note that the change was made slowly throughout the Middle Ages in Europe, with a number of countries adhering to different dates through the fifteenth century.

The Julian calendar (JC), an ultimate refinement of the RC, was attributed to Julius Caesar in 46 BCE. The JC set a regular calendar year of 365 days and 12 months, adding a leap day every four years and aiming to closely follow the solar calendar. The GC—what we know today as "our" calendar—was introduced in 1582 CE by then-Pope Gregory and named for him. The primary purposes of the GC were to retouch the JC and, most importantly, to calculate a regular occurrence for the Christian Easter.

What's important here is knowing that the dates and traditions of the New Year have changed over time, as have the celebrations. Today, the New Year is typically a time for celebration, parties, and fireworks. Many religious communities observe

New Year's Eve as "Watch Night," gathering together to send the old year out and watch the new one in.

The ancient Egyptians threw a huge party on the Nile Delta to celebrate the New Year, complete with barges piled with shrines and offerings. People in the United States tune in to watch the "ball drop" in Times Square—or attend in person if they're able. Mexicans celebrate New Year's Eve by eating a grape with each of the twelve chimes of the final countdown, while the Portuguese eat twelve raisins—one for each month of the year. The French celebrate with an all-out feast.

Scotland may have one of the most interesting traditions in their Hogmanay, which spill out of private homes and fill the streets. The term *Hogmanay* may be a corruption of *au gui menez*, "lead to the mistletoe," suggesting a Druidic history for the feasting, as Britain's Druidic priests usually cut the sacred mistletoe around the Winter Solstice. Matthews also suggests the term may have come from an old Celtic song that began *oge midne*, "new morning" (Matthews, 188). In any case, the term *Hogmanay* has become synonymous with the New Year and with a blowout party, Scottish style.

Another well-known Scottish New Year tradition is that of "first footing." In its simplest form, it is said that the first visitor to the home in the New Year portends the home's luck for the following year. To have a dark-haired man visit is said to bring the best luck. A more elaborate version has all lights in the house being put out at midnight, except for a single candle flame. A family member is sent outside with the flame and must prevent it from going out. At midnight, the person knocks on the door and is welcomed in by everyone within the house. The "guest" then goes around the house and uses the candle to ceremonially relight the home. It's easy to see the connections between this ritual and the "return of light" themes common to solstice celebrations.

In another variation, the "first foot" brings along a lump of coal for good luck. Scottish tradition also requires the "foot" to bring a bottle of alcohol, usually Scotch whisky—which, by the way, is the traditional beverage with which to toast the New Year, along with the singing of the Scottish *Aulde Lang Syne*. Other traditional gifts include shortbread, fruitcake, and black bun (a very dark-colored fruitcake). Once the "first foot" has entered and been welcomed, the festivities begin, with singing, dancing, and much food and drink. Eggnog is traditionally served at this time.

These "old ways" of Midwinter—gods and goddesses, gifts, merriment, lights, the promise of life renewed, homages to the sun, and the inevitable celebrations—continue to touch us today, guided as they are by the inexorable movements of sun, heavens, and the great seasonal Wheel.

NEW WAYS

...pression, ...song, insight, search for meaning sacrifice, silence

and looking inward, evaluation, reflection, meditation, hibernat...

...nd scrying, study, journaling, tool crafting, feasting, commun...

...rk, deep ritual, vigil personal retreat, Amaterasu, Baba Ya...

Bruno, Cailleach, Carlin, Carravogue, Ceres, Demeter, Decim...

...e Koliada, Lachesis, Marzanna, Rind, Skadi, Sneguroc...

...olues, Holler, Lugh, Saturn, Dilis Varsvlavi, Cert, Ebe...

Knight, Green Man, Holly King, Karkantzaros, Knecht

...tzelfrau, Pelznichol, Perchta, Samichlaus, Stallo, Tomten,

...Egregores, green: evergreen, abundance, life, new beginnings, we...

...lth, gifts, prosperity, solar energy, red: holly berries and poin...

...fire, white: silence, calm peace, protecting, cardamom: divin...

...sm, psychic powers, cinnamon: access to astral and spiritual

...ion strength, cloves: attraction, authority, healing power, prote...

intuition, renewal, transformation, vitality, mistletoe: peace, pr...

protection, nutmeg, alertness, awareness, inspiration, intelligenc...

calm, divination, intuition, psychic powers, relaxation, rosemary...

...shing, divination, healing, mental clarity, physical and psych...

...trength, sage: calm concentration, confidence, health and healin...

$\mathcal{I}$N THIS CHAPTER we'll explore Midwinter from a more modern perspective. What does it mean to be a winter-celebrating Pagan today? Only a few of us still live our lives as farmers—so why do we continue to follow the Wheel of the Year, which is an agricultural calendar? What are the symbols of winter, and how do modern Pagans and others embrace the season? How do our fellow humans, magickal and mundane, celebrate Midwinter? Where are the connections between our ancient past and our modern practices? And what does it mean when modern Pagans talk about Yule?

Celebrating an Ancient Holiday in a Modern World

These are the days when it's dark when one gets up and dark when one arrives home at day's end. These are days for wearing sweaters, making pots of soup and baked apples, curling up with a good book and a cup of tea, and enjoying a fire in the fireplace. During this time, many folks make the seasonal changes in their homes that tell them winter is arriving: flannel sheets on the beds, winter-colored towels in the bathroom, a new altar arrangement, special tablecloths, soaps scented with rosemary and juniper, warming tea blends, and a crystal wreath that evokes an indoor burst of snow and ice.

The ways modern cultures celebrate Midwinter are as varied as they are fascinating—and most include at least some of the recurrent symbols that we associate with Pagan Midwinter traditions, such as gift giving, birth, feasting, concepts of peace and goodwill, and above all, lights and the return of the sun.

In Japan, the solstice period is known as *Toji*. Many Japanese take vacations during this time and engage in ceremonies that include bonfires, pumpkin eating (pumpkins are believed to bring luck), and the honoring of ancestors. On the actual solstice, bonfires are lit on Mt. Fuji—Japan's highest mountain—to welcome the return of the rising sun, Japan's national symbol.

Las Posadas (December 16–24) is a nine-day Midwinter celebration held throughout Mexico. The high point of the festivities is a procession of "pilgrims," who walk through a village or neighborhoods and knock at doors asking for *posada* (shelter). This commemorates the search by Joseph and Mary for a shelter in which the infant Jesus—their holy child, a symbol of light and renewal—might be born. It is yet another reference to the theme of new life in winter. The pilgrims are invited inside, and fun and merrymaking ensue with blindfolded guests trying to break a piñata (a papier-mâché decorated earthenware figure filled with gifts and goodies) suspended from the ceiling. Once the piñata is broken, the gifts are distributed and the party starts.

Iranians celebrate the longest night of the year as *Yalda*. The ceremony has an Indo-Iranian origin, where light and good were considered to struggle against darkness and evil. With fires burning and lights lit, family and friends gather to stay up through the night helping the sun in its battle against darkness. They recite poetry, tell stories, and eat special fruits and nuts until the sun, triumphant, reappears in the morning.

In China, under the old monarchies, December 22 was the day in which the emperor led an annual round of sacrifices to the gods. These rituals were secret, and little knowledge remains about them. In today's China, many still treat the solstice as a holiday, feasting and making offerings to the sacred ancestors.

And of course, Yule is significant and even sacred to many Pagan religious festivals today. Although the descriptions and connections vary, these festivals typically contains clear references to the cyclic Wheel of the Year and to the symbols we associate with Midwinter.

For Wiccans, the holiday is known as Yule and generally takes place on the solstice eve and day itself. A Wiccan Yule ritual typically involves casting a circle; calling the four quarters, directions, or watchtowers; raising energy; and doing focused work with a deity. A Yule log is often a central focus, and the ritual may emphasize workings for peace, goodwill, and a prosperous New Year. Appeals and offerings are made to mother goddesses, and ideas of rebirth and new light take center stage.

Witches in the Reclaiming tradition may or may not use structured ritual, and if they do, it will look like a typical Wiccan ritual. The most important difference in a Reclaiming Yule is the intentional keeping of vigil over a Yule log fire through the solstice night, after which they midwife the rising sun's rebirth. They follow this with "singing up the sun" at dawn.

Heathens—who celebrate Norse traditions—use many of the familiar symbols of Yule, but they celebrate Midwinter as a twelve-day festival—the Twelve Nights of Yule—beginning on or around the Winter Solstice and ending on January 1 (note: timeline may vary depending on the starting date). Each night focuses on a specific activity, with some done in the Kindred (a group of Heathens who practice together) and some done individually or with one's family. Gifts may be given on each night. Some of the activities include:

Decorating with greenery—including a Yule tree.

Dream divination—dreams experienced during the twelve days are felt to be prophetic of the coming year; dreams are tracked by journaling.

Hoodening—dressing in animals skins or masks and acting out
   plays, dances, and processions, or parading with animal effigies, skulls, etc.

Mummering, Morris dancing, and sword dancing—similar to
   Morris dancing, sword dancing involves a carefully choreographed dance with swords, usually with lots of leap-
   ing and clashing. The sword dance often concludes with a
   mock beheading, followed by a ceremonial resurrection.

Wassailing—carrying wassail from house to house and using it
   to bless fruit trees, ensuring a bountiful harvest in the coming year.

Burning a Yule log—this was traditionally brought in on Mother's Night and, for the best luck and fortune in the New
   Year, was burned on each of the Twelve Nights of Yule.

   Pagans embracing Celtic Reconstructionism or Celtic Re-
constructionist Druidism typically don't celebrate at the Winter Solstice. They believe this occasion was not marked by the
ancient Druids, who only recognized the four fire festivals (Imbolc, Beltane, Lughnasadh, and Samhain) and marked Samhain
as the start of winter. However, folkloric recording tell us that
the Celtic peoples did celebrate Midwinter and, with incoming

Christianization, Christmas as well. For instance, the Scottish people typically celebrated the winter season and Christmas beginning on December 12 and continuing for at least a month (Hopman, 69). During this time, much of the normal household work ceased and could not resume until the Yule feast was over—typically around January 11–12. Kevin Danaher tells us that for the Irish, Midwinter and the Christmas season were among the year's most important times (Danaher, 233–243). Irish houses, barns, and farmyards were scrubbed clean before the holiday. Homes were festooned with greenery and each home had a special log to burn on Christmas Eve—the *blog na nollag*. Candles were lit on Christmas Eve: one for each family member. Christmas Eve was a fasting day, but on Christmas itself, grand feasts were held, and the greatest gifts to share with neighbors were those of the finest foodstuffs. Christmas Day began with church and then was spent snuggled in with one's family.

Modern eclectic Druids often honor the solstice, rationalizing that the solstices were key astronomical events that would have been observed by the Druids and other learned people. These solstice rituals often involve a procession to the ritual location; the raising of energy; the making of offerings to the three realms of land, sea, and sky; the making of offerings to gods, ancestors, and nature spirits; welcoming and interaction with a deity; and an act of divination or reading of omens to intuit the results of the ritual.

In each of these examples, we see recurrent themes: work with light, references to the sun's return, and appeals for peace and well-being. We're also not surprised to see the trappings and decor of the season used throughout the rituals, including evergreens, candles, music, and celebratory feasting: cakes and ale typically are no holds barred at Midwinter. Gift giving, game playing, and other expressions of joyful celebration are common parts of Yule ritual, too.

The Natural World at Yule

Departing from the richly sculpted "landscape" of formal ritual, the classic winter landscape is likewise unmistakable. Deciduous trees have lost their leaves and stand skeletal, while evergreen branches are heavily weighted by rain, snow, and ice. A layer of snow may cover the landscape, insulating the earth against the coolest temperatures and providing protection for plants, insects, and other animals. The edges of rivers and creeks may freeze and lakes and ponds may freeze over as well, but the water underneath remains fluid, allowing aquatic life to be sustained. Some animals hibernate while others sink into a reduced metabolic state known as torpor. Still others must live through the winter, doing their best to survive—and not all will succeed.

The landscape is at once harsh and gorgeous, and above all, it's silent. The clean, cold night air and short days make for brilliantly clear night skies and extraordinary views of stars, meteors, and perhaps even the northern lights, if one lives in the right location. The snow-covered landscape creates an aura of purity and peacefulness. There is a sense that the earth is sleeping and that the natural world is gathering force and working quiet magick as it awaits the coming of spring.

Now, granted, your own winter landscape may vary. The closer you live to the equator, the less you'll experience in terms of seasonal temperature and light variations. Conversely, the farther you are from the equator, the more profound these changes will be. But even if you live in a locale that's warm and sunny all year or one where weeks of rain are the rule and snow never falls, you'll still be able to find seasonal variations—if you pay attention. Study the landscape around you. What is in leaf or blooming? What birds and animals are around, and which ones have either migrated or begun hibernation? How long are the days? What stars and planets are wheeling by overhead? Try to get outside every day to make your own winter experience stronger.

Why is this important to us as magick users? Winter is a time of resilience. It's a time to looks deep within and find strength, nurturing one's inner spark and keeping it safe and warm throughout the cold months. But let's not over-romanticize this. Wintertime is tough. Weather changes, cold, snow and ice, and a lack of food can be lethal, and only the strongest and most adaptive plants and creatures survive. Likewise, many people today struggle with seasonable affective disorder during the winter months. In a way both real and metaphorical, winter is one of nature's limiting factors—a way to ensure survival of the fittest. But out of those struggles come courage, strength, and self-reliance.

We modern humans, too, can capitalize on using winter to reach down, find strength, and emerge renewed come springtime. Midwinter has so much to offer if we only reach out and grasp it. Being an active part of winter—rather than avoiding it—is an essential part of this. Make winter your friend—your seasonal partner.

The Symbols of Midwinter

Our modern Midwinter celebrations are rich with symbolic representations of the season—most with ancient connections. When we bring these images into our own homes and festivities, we can feel the connections with times past, enriching the observances and making them ever more wondrous. The symbols make our surroundings more beautiful and inspire our magicks. Not only that, but embracing these tangible representations of season is just plain fun, too.

Birth and Renewal

As we discussed in the chapter *Old Ways*, most traditions at Yule feature a theme of death, birth, or renewal, and this is often expressed as a holy child of some sort, giving us hope that life will renew itself as the Wheel of the Year continues to turn. The solstice brings the return of light—life reborn anew from the earth's womb as a child of light, whether that child be a human infant, a bear hibernating in its winter den, the constellation Orion creeping above the winter horizon, or something else birthed new during the season.

Candles

Candles remind us of the return of the light, for one small candle can light up a completely darkened room. They're a powerful magickal tool, too, for a lit candle works with all four elements simultaneously. Candles are often an important part of magick, ritual, and a seasonal atmosphere, particularly in traditional holiday colors (red, green, gold, or white) or scented with holiday herbs and spices, such as frankincense, cedar, or cinnamon.

Colors

The reds and greens we associate with Yule represent the gifts of the evergreens and berries that flourish during the season. Gold is often linked to Yule, primarily symbolizing the sun but also as a hint to Midwinter's symbolic riches and gifts. White is a sign of purity and of the silence that snow brings to the world. White also is highly reflective, almost creating its own light during the depths of solstice time.

Evergreens

Because they remain green and vital all year, evergreens are a symbol of life, strength, perseverance, and protection during the harshness of winter. We decorate our homes with evergreen swags, wreaths, and trees, festooning the greens with ribbons and decorations as a way of invoking this ancient protective gift. Greens fill the home with instant aromatherapy, too. Even if you use artificial greens, you're still capturing the evergreen essence. For extra oomph, dress your artificial greens with a few drops of essential conifer oil.

Feasting

For the ancients, winter was a terrifying time, a time when they had to live off food and fuel stored during the warmer months and pray that it would be enough. The coming of the Winter Solstice meant a renewed chance of survival, and it was typically honored with the best feast the people could muster. Solstice feasting has thus become symbolic of bounty, celebration, gratitude, and optimism. Whether planning a party, a daily meal, or a grand holiday feast, don't be afraid to embrace the season and go over the top with a really splendid dish or a dizzying array of offerings. The *Recipes and Crafts* chapter in this book will give you some good ideas for your own celebratory feasts.

Gifts

Gift giving is a focal symbol of many winter traditions. Giving gifts shows that we care for each other's well-being and are committed to helping each other survive the long, cold winter. It shows our willingness to share our own good fortune with others. These kinds of communal actions provide a deep meaning to our experience of the solstice season and bring us together. They also remind us to care for one another; it takes a village to make it through a winter. The best kind of gift giving reaches out to others; many families make a tradition of doing community service during the winter holidays.

Guising

The act of disguising oneself as an animal, or guising, allowed aboriginal humans to honor symbolic or totem animals and to enact the idea of sacrifice by becoming symbolically related to the animals that sustained them through the winter. In slightly later times, processions of animal guisers likewise found their way into the winter rituals of many cultures. Guising still goes on today, usually in conjunction with mummery and Morris dancing. It is also a common practice to create animal effigies—particularly from sheaves of grains and straw—to carry throughout winter celebrations as a means of appealing for fertility and bounty.

Herbs and Spices

Cedar, fir, cinnamon, cardamom, and peppermint are some of the welcomed smells of the season. Dress candles with essential oils; infuse herbs into tea, coffee, or hot chocolate; put out bowls of potpourri; simmer herbs and sliced citrus in a kettle of water on the stove top; drip essential oils into your bathwater.

Lights

If the Winter Solstice is about anything, it's about light, whether the light of our hearth and home, the light of renewed life, the light of our hearts, or the light of the returning sun. Light may be represented by everything from candles to firelight to strands of glittering tinsel to holiday lights to the sun itself. Today, most magickal and many nonmagickal cultures hold some sort of celebration around the time of the Winter Solstice, and most of them feature light. For example, there is the Jewish celebration of Hanukkah, the Christian midnight candle mass, or the Pagan idea of sitting by a vigil fire awaiting the solstice sunrise. An oft-repeated tale of Midwinter light is that of Raven, credited by many North American aboriginal traditions as both trickster and bringer of light, as in this Tlingit version:

A long time ago, the Raven looked down from the sky and saw that the people of the world were living in darkness. The ball of light was kept hidden by a selfish old chief. So the Raven turned itself into a spruce needle and floated on the river where the chief's daughter came for water. She drank the spruce needle. She became pregnant and gave birth to a boy, which was the Raven in disguise. The baby cried and cried until the chief gave him the ball of light to play with. As soon as he had the light, the Raven turned back into himself and carried the light into the sky. From then on, we no longer lived in darkness. (Swanton)

To see a wonderful folkloric expression of this Raven myth, complete with gorgeous northwest coastal art, watch the television show *Northern Exposure*, season 3, episode 25, entitled "Seoul Mates." Search the Web for a three minute YouTube video of the Raven pageant at the show's end, guaranteed to help you "feel" the season.

Magickal Animals

Magickal animals have a key place in Yule lore. Consider the Wild Hunt rushing by on a stormy night, the Great Bear wheeling by in the starry skies overhead, or the magickal reindeer that pull Santa's sleigh. The Irish believe that on Christmas Eve, cows and donkeys kneel down in adoration of the Christ child and are also able to speak at this time (Danaher, 239). Animals also play traditional roles in many Midwinter tableaus.

Deer, for instance, appear in winter stories and myths throughout the magickal world. They are strongly associated with winter, particularly as objects of the hunt. Known to be shy creatures, deer are regarded as both solitary and herd animals. Much of their activity is nocturnal, earning them a reputation as one of the night's gentle ghosts. Since deer don't hibernate and must forage through the winter, they have long been an important food source during the cold months.

The male deer, or stag, remains sacred to the dark season as a symbol of the Horned God, who reigns during winter. One variation is the Anglo-Saxon *Woden*, who is often shown wearing horns as he gallops along with the Wild Hunt. Speaking of horns, the "King Stag" is one of the strongest of archetypal male symbols, and the old kings were often crowned with antlers, as told in the Arthurian legends. In more Shamanistic cultures, the medicine man or woman may wear antlers to invoke the forest god or the totemic animal itself, insuring a good hunting season for the upcoming year. Some of the oldest known masks found among aboriginal tribes in the United States are of deer and elk.

Deer can also be found bounding through the ancient stories of Egypt, Greece, India, and much of Indo-European myth. In Celtic tradition, deer often appear as magickal beings during the Wild Hunt, where they mark entry into the faerie realm or serve as a transfigured form for otherworldly women. Today's magick users revere the stag as a symbol of pride, strength, and virility, as well as a focus of consecration or purification.

The deer is also sacred to the Winter Solstice because of a belief that the stag carries the sun in his antlers. Symbolically, deer antlers resemble tree branches, and like tree branches, the antlers are shed and regrown each year in a real-life example of rebirth and rejuvenation.

Cows and oxen are important winter symbols of food and wealth for people in sub-Arctic climes. The period around the Winter Solstice marks the traditional time of the "culling of the herds," when animals are selected out of the herd to be slaughtered for food. It's no accident that a stately prime rib of beast is a traditional, celebratory roast still served for winter holidays.

Pigs, too, are stars of Midwinter. Pigs are very intelligent and were long considered powerful, sacred animals. The ancient Celts believed pigs to be a gift from the otherworld, and the Norse god of sunshine, Frey, rode across the sky on the back of a gold-bristled boar, *Gulli-burstin*, whose spikey bristles looked like the sun's rays. Pigs often make a star appearance on Midwinter feast tables (crown roast of pork, anyone?) and are also part of an ancient sacrificial ritual known as "Bringing in the Boar," in which a wild boar's head is paraded through the people as a sort of winter sacrifice. This is likely what gave rise to the tradition of serving a suckling pig as part of a traditional English holiday feast. The parading of the boar's head still takes place every year at Queen's College, Oxford, and likely in other locales as well.

Those who prefer not to park an entire creature on a serving plate may create a boar effigy; one might start with a cheese ball or a small ham, sticking it with toothpick bristles on which are impaled cubes of meat or cheese. Using toothpicks, olives can be affixed as eyes, with a piece of red pepper to create a mouth. The "boar" may be placed on a platter, garnished with greens, herbs, and candles, and paraded around the room as a nontraditional culinary sacrifice.

The horse is also sacred to many cultures. Matthews describes a Midwinter ritual known as *hoodening*, in which a man costumed as a horse goes door-to-door, collecting money in exchange for entertainment. The hooden-horse was carried by several men, known as *hoodeners*. "Coins were placed in the horse's mouth and in return the hooden offered blessings and wise sayings—hence the term, 'from the horse's mouth' (Matthews, 155)." Legend suggests that "Robin Hood bled to death on Yule Eve and reappeared as a hobbyhorse," leading to a tradition (as recently as the 1700s) of "bleeding" horses on Yule Eve as a means of ensuring their good health (Hopman, 69).

The bear is also a potent player in the games of Midwinter. The bear is revered throughout many traditional cultures as the symbol of winter incarnate, for when bears emerge from their period of winter hibernation, light and life have clearly returned to the earth. And in the Northern Hemisphere, the asterism Ursa Major—the Great Bear—wheels overhead during the winter months.

Mistletoe

Mistletoe is a parasitic plant that grows on other trees and woody shrubs—particularly on oak trees. The ancient Druids harvested mistletoe at Yule with great ceremony, believing it to be a holy plant with protective qualities. It is one of few plants that flowers during the winter months, and during Saturnalia fertility rituals took place under bowers of mistletoe—perhaps the reason for the modern tradition of kissing underneath it. Our use of mistletoe today recalls these traditions. But be warned: mistletoe is poisonous when taken internally.

Peace and Well-Being

The idea that people can be sustained through the winter safely and peacefully, in comfort and free of danger, is at the heart of Midwinter lore and ritual. The winter holidays seem to bring people together in a shared effort for survival, and during these dark months, many set aside their frustrations and ill will for the communal benefits of making it through winter.

Sun

To people of Earth, the sun is everything. The sun is, in the most literal fashion, responsible for both light and life, for without its energies to drive photosynthesis and give rise to plant life, nothing on Earth would survive. We honor that at the solstices, as the sun moves through its annual circle.

Tribalism

There will always be people who, for whatever reason, find themselves alone at Yule or choose to celebrate holidays alone. But most Yule festivities are absolutely aimed at communal celebration—a time to celebrate connections between family, friends, and community. For magickal folks, this could mean public or private ritual, a splendid feast, or an evening of storytelling around the fire, mugs of wassail in hand. However we celebrate Yule, we do so with the understanding that we are part of a larger whole.

The Great Tree Debate

Those who love to bring in a cut tree for the holidays point to the traditions of death and sacrifice that abound at Yule, as well as the fact that cutting and decorating a tree or bough is a tradition that goes back thousands of years. Others feel that tradition or not, it's wrong to cut a living tree simply for the purpose of creating a seasonal decoration or focal point. These folks either go with an artificial tree or do without. Some people choose a happy medium, bringing a potted living tree into the home temporarily, just for the holiday period, and then returning it to the outdoors.

Whatever the reasoning, artificial trees are on the upswing today and gaining in popularity. Artificial trees are increasingly more attractive and "real" looking, and, once purchased, can be used year after year. Most artificial trees are made in China, while natural trees are primarily grown in the western United States.

Interestingly, while most artificial trees were once made of aluminum, they're now mostly made of plastics and resins. The process of creating these trees creates a large proportion of toxic by-products in relation to the end result, and also involves lead in the production—particularly when "built-in" fiber optic lights are permanently attached to the trees. The fine print in these instances often advises users to touch the tree only when wearing gloves!

Those of us who like trees are faced with choices: should we have a tree or not? If we have one, should it be a live tree, a sacrificed tree, or a fake tree? It's a choice that must be made individually, but consider some of the following, from the National Christmas Tree Association website:

- Every acre of trees on a Christmas tree farm provides enough oxygen for eighteen people.
- For each Christmas tree that is harvested, three seedlings are planted.
- In one year, an average mature evergreen tree produces enough oxygen to support a family of four and absorbs the carbon dioxide pumped into the air by four automobiles.
- Planting trees is the cheapest, most effective way of removing excess carbon dioxide from the atmosphere.
- Unsold trees are composted into mulch, bark dust, and compost.

Decorating your tree should be just plain fun—you can make it into an official "event" by serving refreshments or even a tree-trimming meal. According to tradition, you should take down your Christmas tree and decorations on Twelfth Night, January 5, for to take the tree down earlier is to fail to honor the solstice evergreen for its gifts. However, you may need to take your tree down earlier if it becomes dangerously dry. It's more important to not let your house burn down than to follow ancient custom!

When you do take your tree down, do so with ceremony and thanks. Wrap up a reusable tree or dispose of a natural tree with respectful reverence. Some people place the tree in their yard for a time, decorating it with offerings for the birds and critters. Others take their tree to a recycler or cut the pieces up to dry for a ritual bonfire later on in the year. Be sure to cut a nice portion of the trunk for next year's Yule Log.

The Prevailing Energies and Energetics of Yule

Many people these days—including Pagans—express dislike for winter's cold, darkness, rain, snow, and long nights and wish aloud, fervently, for the return of summer. Granted, winter presents its challenges, but it also holds unique gifts—gifts that are pure gold to Pagans and other magickal folk, and gifts that have much to teach. For those who are not generally fond of winter, there is much to be gained by simply adopting a fresh, resolute perspective and plunging into an intentional experience of the Midwinter season. This can be an important part of one's personal goal-setting and magickal practices.

One of winter's greatest gifts is that of quiet: a feeling of silence, calmness, inward-drawing, and introspection. It's a chance to pull out of the hustle and bustle of daily life and slow down. It's time to read, to think, to nap, to ponder, to hunker down in our metaphorical cave and while the winter away. Doing this take intention and resolution—it requires effort to say to oneself, "Winter isn't the same as summer, and I can't treat it the same." It means that one's days, meals, and sleep patterns should be different. Because, winter is *different*. We can only experience this deep quiet by allowing ourselves to fall into sync with the new rhythms.

Another gift of winter is that of renewal: the fresh start. Midwinter is a kind of metaphorical sleep or even, in some traditions, a kind of symbolic death. But as with each turning of the Wheel, sleep is followed by an awakening and death by renewed life. During winter, we take stock, think consciously about what to finish or leave behind (what must "die," so to speak) and, conversely, what to pick up or begin anew.

Along the same lines, winter gives us *time*: quiet, unhurried time to take stock of the past months and evaluate what transpired. What worked? What didn't? What goals were realized, and which ones weren't? And most importantly, what do we want to do in the year to come? With the evaluation complete, goal setting can begin. Using a computer, a journal, a bulletin board with notes and pushpins, or whatever system works best for you, chart a path for the year to come, setting goals for a week, a month, six months, etc. Plan for the coming rebirth and renewal.

Winter challenges us to learn to adapt. There will always come times when one must cope with an unfamiliar, difficult, or even dangerous setting, whether in magickal or mundane life. In such instances, winter teaches us to be strong, persistent, clever, and wary, combining a clear understanding of our resources with the ability to watch for sudden opportunity. We're encouraged to modify our usual routines to fit the special needs of winter as well as finding ways to keep going throughout an often-challenging season. Winter is a different time, and it calls, sensibly, for a different lifestyle. You might ask yourself this: what parts of my routine do I need to change or adapt in order to have am enjoyable, healthful, and productive winter, one filled with personal growth?

And of course, winter's greatest gift is that of celebration—joyous celebration with family, friends, and community in magick, not to be missed.

A Conundrum: Calendar Versus Convenience

For most of us, our lives are more or less ruled by the modern calendar, and sooner or later, we must grapple with the question of "calendar versus convenience." Let's imagine your coven or grove wants to hold a significant ritual on the Winter Solstice, and you're hoping for all of your members to participate. But alas: the solstice happens to fall on Thursday this year, and many of your members are tied up with work, family, or other obligations on Thursday night. Is it acceptable to shift the ritual to the following Saturday night?

There is no clear answer to this question (if you were hoping for one, sorry). Some purists insist on holding events on the "correct day," and in some cases—as when doing deeply religious ritual, making offerings to a specific deity, focusing on an uncommon astronomical alignment, or something similar—it is necessary to cleave to a specific date and time. On the other hand, an event may be better attended if it is shifted slightly to accommodate peoples' schedules. Thus, many circles, groves, covens, and other groups move celebrations and even rituals to dates when more of their members are available, and this can be quite successful. This is a decision you and your group must make together, with the group's best interests considered alongside the magickal needs. For best results, make plans early and publicize them well.

Another Conundrum: The Merging of Traditions

Most people who follow some sort of Pagan tradition find that the Wheel of the Year serves them well as a reliable guide to season and practice, thanks to its connections to nature and the living earth. However, particularly in these modern times, people often find themselves splicing celebrations together to meet individual needs of self, family, and friends. For instance, many Pagans who observe Yule also celebrate other December holidays, such as Christmas, Chanukah, or Diwali.

I know that's true of me: my family, some of whom are not Pagan, has always celebrated Christmas, although we do so in a way that focuses on cultural/secular symbols and longstanding traditions rather than religion. As it turns out, our "Christmas" celebrations end up looking quite Pagan, and in my house, Christmas and Yule seem to merge smoothly into one long, lovely winter holiday season. As for you? Consider what is meaningful to you in terms of family, religion or spirituality, and culture, then think about how you view and wish to celebrate the idea of winter, using these ideas to design the perfect celebration.

For instance, if you find beauty in certain aspects of Christmas, capture those ideas and merge them with your Midwinter activities. It seems clear that the Winter Solstice, in all its guises, has long been celebrated as more of a "holiday season" than as a single day. Modern practitioners of Wicca, Witchcraft, Druidism, Heathenism, and other similar traditions use Yule, Yuletide, and Midwinter as descriptive terms for the Pagan religious festivals that take place on or around the time of the Winter Solstice. In this way, we touch centuries (perhaps millennia) of traditions that have gone before. The point of the season, after all, is that it brings us joy and brings us closer to our loved ones and perhaps our gods. How we arrive at that point is up to us.

There's one more point I'd like to address before we move on. Some of you reading this may still be all or partly "in the broom closet" and may not be comfortable revealing your Pagan traditions to your family or friends, and this can create challenges for you. But in the case of Yule, you're in luck, for the symbolism of Midwinter is so consistent across most traditions and cultures, it's possible to set up an altar or a shrine, decorate a solstice tree, carry out a ritual or magickal working, and sing Pagan-oriented carols "in plain sight," with no one the wiser. Some will see "Christmas," but, if you'll forgive the pun, Yule see Yule. I call this win-win.

Some Final Reflections

Let's return to some of the questions that opened this chapter...

What does it mean to be a winter-celebrating Pagan today? It means honoring the power and gifts of the season—which are unique and distinct from those expressed during other times of the year. It means considering the lessons winter can teach us and embracing them rather than trying to escape or deny them. It means looking deep to see the true beauty of the season.

Only a few of us still live our lives as farmers—so why do we continue to follow an agricultural calendar like the Wheel of the Year? We do this because these traditions tie us to the past and to the ancient peoples who followed the same rhythms. This evokes nostalgia and gives our lives depth and richness. As magickal folks, the seasonal Wheel provides a sort of rudder, helping us steer a strong course through the year's changing seasons and showing us how the seasons work and flow together to keep the world turning.

What are the symbols of winter, and how do modern Pagans and others embrace the season? We experience the beauty of the season through links to past, present, and future with lights, color, greenery, gifts, feasting, and more.

How do our fellow humans, magickal and mundane, celebrate Midwinter? And where are the connections between our ancient past and our modern practices? By understanding the rituals and lore of Yule and their magickal applications, we bring the old and the new into our practices, creating a personalized approach to the holiday that honors tradition while embracing modernity.

And what does it mean when modern Pagans talk about Yule? It means magick!

SPELLS
AND
DIVINATION

...compassion, wisdom, insight, search for meaning, sacrifice, ...

...tion and looking inward, evaluation, reflection, meditation, hibe...

...on and scrying, study, journaling, tool crafting, feasting, comm...

...work, deep ritual, vigil, personal retreat, Amaterasu, Baba...

...a, Bríine, Cailleach, Carlin, Carravogue, Ceres, Demeter, ...

...olda, Koliada, Lachesis, Marzana, Rind, Skadi, Snegu...

...Bacchus, Hodhr, Lugh, Saturn, Dílis Varsolar, Cert, ...

...en Knight, Green Man, Holly King, Karkantzaros, Kna...

...Lutzelfrau, Pelznichol, Perchta, Samichlaus, Stallo, ...

...ann, Egregores, green: evergreen, abundance, life, new beginning...

...wealth, gifts, prosperity, solar energy, red: holly berries and ...

...force, fire, white: silence, calm peace, protecting, cardamom: ...

...ticism, psychic powers, cinnamon: access to astral and spirit...

...tuition strength, cloves: attraction, authority, healing power, ...

...th, intuition, renewal, transformation, vitality, mistletoe: powe...

...st, protection, nutmeg, alertness, awareness, inspiration, intell...

...nt, calm, divination, intuition, psychic powers, relaxation, rose...

...banishing, divination, healing, mental clarity, physical and ...

...a strength, sage: calm concentration, confidence, health and ...

*F*OR THOSE WHO follow Pagan traditions, magick is an important part of both practice and daily life, and the winter season is a valuable part of our annual cycle of practices. It's inspired by the changes many of us see at winter. Anyone who has grown up in a snowy clime knows the feeling of waking up one morning and seeing the world suddenly different, as if nature waved a giant magick wand over the landscape and everything changed. All disruption and all dysfunction disappear under a blanket of pure white. The quiet beauty of winter fairly inspires magick, and in this chapter, we'll explore some inspiring ways to craft a magickal winter.

Magickal Timing

Magickal timing is always a key part of working any magick, and it's worth considering day, month, moon phase, astrological cycle, and whatever other markers are meaningful to you.

During the morning hours, the sun takes charge of the world and we experience "waxing" (growing) energy. This is an excellent time to conclude a Yule ritual or vigil, to carry out magicks aimed at "growth" or expansion, or to undertake creative work, such as making gifts or seasonal decorations.

Midday is a time of balance. We imagine noon with the sun directly overhead, but in winter, the sun simply doesn't rise that high. Still, at noon, the sun's power reaches its peak and even given winter's short days, noon brings an implied balance between day and night. Use this time for ritual or magicks that work with solar energies, renewal, or divination. It's also an excellent time of day for reading or quiet contemplation.

During the afternoon, the sun's energy begins to wane (ebb) as it moves toward sunset. During the summer months, the direct, intense sunlight warms the earth and creates hot afternoons and warm evenings; during winter, with a lower and less intense sun, the earth begins to cool almost immediately as the sun drops to the horizon. Capitalize on this when working with evaluation, introspection, journaling, or planning. Winter afternoons are a wonderful time to take walks and likewise are the perfect time for natural augury, i.e., identifying and interpreting naturally occurring signs and omens.

Sunset takes place when the sun drops below the horizon. Darkness and chill come quickly after a winter sunset and are followed by a short dusk (also called twilight). The sun's energies fade rapidly, giving way to a clear, crisp night sky. This "liminal" time—standing between day and night—is deeply

SPELLS AND DIVINATION

magickal, making it a good time to work with charms and spells or to appeal to or petition deities. (But work quickly: at Midwinter, this in-between time vanishes in minutes.)

During the dark of night, vision diminishes and one must rely on the other senses. Temperatures fall swiftly, particularly in winter. Night is an ideal time to work with winter's dynamic darkness and to address fears, challenges, and obstacles. The clear skies make night a very good time for divination and meditation as well as celestial magicks and sky watching.

Midnight has always been known as "the witching hour," and this is high time for magick of all sorts, particularly as a reference to the darkness and danger of winter. The same goes for the late night, which is a kind of "happy hour" for sprites, faeries, and spirit visitations.

Also, consider the idea of the "eve," which refers to the night before an important event. An eve is an incredibly powerful time magickally. It implies not only a balance—between what has happened and what is about to come—but also creates a tension between past, present, and future. An eve is a time of both transition and threshold, a potent time for magickal or spiritual work, especially reflective work and divination. The power inherent in this time shows clearly in the number of mainstream churches that feature midnight or evening services on Christmas Eve.

Winter Spellcraft

Good spellwork tantalizes the senses, touching on sight, smell, touch, taste, and sound. For starters, winter offers us a full bouquet of magickal colors to work with. Silver and gold (or yellow) are reminiscent of the season's riches as well as the shining ones (our ancestors) and the brilliance of the sun's return. Red is reminiscent of winterberries, while green reminds us of glorious evergreens, and blue of the crisp, clear winter day. White is all around us in the form of winter snow and ice, and black evokes the crystalline night sky. And what about brown? You might relate it to the earth, sleeping beneath the snow. As for me: I'm thinking about chocolate! (Every season is a good one for chocolate, as far as I'm concerned.)

And smell? Consider the bite of a juniper bough, the acrid smell of a burning fire, the warmth of cinnamon and nutmeg, and the sharpness of peppermint. Scientists tell us that smell is our most potent memory trigger, able to instantly catapult us decades back, to the scent of our piano teacher's lilac water or the dusty attic in our childhood home. These memory triggers, along with magickal correspondences, make scent a powerful adjunct to winter magicks.

Sound, of course, suggests music, chanting, signing, and the sounds of drums and bells. But imagine, too, the crackling sound of a winter fire or the almost absent sound of snowfall. And textures? Think cold, wet ice; the crunchy sound of crumpled wrapping paper; the waxy texture of cedar boughs; or the smooth oiliness of a candle.

The colors, smells, sounds, and textures of winter are a wonderful part of creating winter spells, charms, talismans, and magicks. Let's start by considering a couple of definitions:

Works of magick may be simple and casual—as when one speaks aloud a quick wish for guidance or protection ("Brigid, be with me now!")—or can involve detailed, carefully crafted spellwork that takes effort and care to set in motion. Anything done in an effort to work with energy or possibility or to invoke the assistance of element or deity is a type of magic.

When preparing to begin any magickal working, start with the following:

1. Ask yourself what you wish to accomplish and why.
2. Be certain of whom you wish to affect with the magick and for how long.
3. Be sure of yourself. Magick works best when one is in good health, well rested, and has the available time to work without feeling rushed.
4. Have a sense of your capabilities—don't try something you aren't ready for.
5. Just as one carries out *mise en place* when cooking, your magick should also begin by gathering materials and making sure all is ready before you begin.

6. Always prepare yourself mentally and physically before working magick. To prepare mentally, you might ground, center, and offer a prayer or appeal. To prepare physically, you might bathe—or at least wash hands and face—and perhaps don special clothing or jewelry that helps you enter "magickal space."

7. Work where you won't be interrupted. Turn off electronics—or better yet, remove them from the room—so you won't be distracted and so the electromagnetic fields do not interfere with your workings.

8. Work slowly, and carefully, keeping your intent in mind throughout the process and concentrating. Focus is very important to effective magick.

9. When finished, either dispose of extra materials using a form of "elemental removal" (e.g., burying in earth, burning, releasing into water—and observing ecological precepts throughout) or store for another use.

We're about to plunge into some specific ideas for spells and divination: feel free to modify any of these for your own needs or intentions. This, after all, is how good magick happens—by personalizing it. You can use the correspondences section at the end of this book for ideas. Let's get started!

Winter House Cleansing and Blessing

The winter holidays typically come with lots of magick, lots of excitement, and lots of company, expected and unexpected. With all of the energies moving in, around, and out of your home, it's a great time to set the stage with a quick house cleansing. Smudge the entryways and corners using sage, sweetgrass, juniper, or cedar, or asperge (sprinkle) with salt water, moving deosil (counterclockwise) from one room to the next. As you work, repeat this:

May the winds inspire you,
earth protect you,
water heal you, and
fire always warm the hearth.

As you move through the space, clap your hands to disperse old, stagnant energy, then use a bell or rattle to welcome in fresh, sacred energy. If you have one or more sleigh bells, they're perfect for this Midwinter cleansing. Open windows to let in fresh air, even if for only a few minutes—this is not only great for cleansing and clarification, but it's also healthful.

Once you've finished the cleansing, bring protective elements into your rooms or hang protective talismans over doors and windows.

- The earth element grounds us and provides a sort of metaphysical "anchor." Place crystals or small bowls of sea salt around the kitchen and evoke crystalline ice and snow. Small ceramic or wooden trees also represent the earth element nicely, as do small animal figurines—particularly Bear, who tunnels into the earth during the winter and then emerges as the light returns.

- The air element is energizing and improves our alertness and mental clarity. Burn incense or simmer a kettle of water and spices on the kitchen stove. Diffuse essential oils. Hang small white lights everywhere or cut paper snowflakes and let them dangle and spin from the ceiling.

- The fire element recalls the spark of life in the so-called dead of winter. To bring in fire burn candles, or if you have a fireplace, make use of it. Set luminarias (see a description in the *Recipes and Crafts* chapter) outside, lighting the path to your door. String lights inside and out—the more, the better! Sip warm mugs of tea, cocoa, or hot cider to kindle your internal fire during the long evenings.

- The water element calms, soothes, and heals. Use mirrors to represent the frozen pools and ice of winter, or set out a small bowl or cauldron of water. Use smooth river rocks to adorn your altars or tableaus.

Variation: use the above ideas to clean and prepare your home on New Year's Day, setting a fresh stage for the year to come.

A Protective Lorica for Yule

This is a "Paganized" version of the traditional Lorica of St. Patrick. A lorica is also referred to as a breastplate—a sort of "word armor" and a traditional petition for protection. Repeat these words upon arising on Winter Solstice morning or upon greeting the solstice sunrise. You could also use this as a daily morning mantra throughout the winter.

> *I arise today*
> *through the strength of the heavens;*
> *light of the sun,*
> *splendor of fire,*
> *clarity of ice,*
> *speed of the wind,*
> *depth of the snow,*
> *stability of the earth,*
> *firmness of the rock.*
> *The light has returned!*

To covert this Lorica into a real breastplate: write the words on a small piece of paper using black ink (for grounding and permanence). Add a few rosemary needles, fold the paper into a secure packet, and tie with a red ribbon (for vitality). Place the packet next to your bed or on your altar where you can see it daily—or, tuck into purse, briefcase, or pocket to keep its protection with you. For extra bling, enclose it in a small magickal bag.

Magickal Bags for Multiple Purposes

Cut two identical pieces of fabric in red, green, gold, or in a holiday print. Put the "right sides" together, then sew around three of the sides; turn the resulting bag right side out. Trim the raw edge with pinking shears and tie shut with a ribbon or a thin cord. These bags can be used to hold items for spells or charms, to safeguard a talisman or small magickal item, for gifts, for dream pillows, or for any number of other purposes.

A Yuletide Dream Pillow

Follow the instructions for "Magickal Bags," above, but after sewing the three sides and turning the bag right side out, fill it with a dried herbal mixture as follows:

- For sleep: lavender and cedar.
- For inspired dreams: mugwort, rosemary, and cloves.
- For psychic inspiration and astral travel: cinnamon and cardamom.

- To make sure Santa will come, try a cookies theme: cinnamon, vanilla, and a dash of sprinkles.

After stuffing, sew the fourth side closed. Tuck the dream pillow inside your pillowcase and enjoy sweet dreams.

A Gingerbread Man Poppet to Safeguard Your Gifts

A poppet—a small figure or effigy stuffed with specific items for magickal purpose—is a potent piece of folk or low magick, and they're wonderful as protective talismans. Use a gingerbread man cookie cutter to cut out two identical shapes in gold felt or other fabric. Decorate the shapes as desired: adding a gold star (sheriff-style) or the crossed belts and sashes of a soldier's outfit will add authority to your wee guard. Sew the two pieces together, leaving a small opening at the top. Stuff the poppet with sage and cinnamon, shredded gift wrap or ribbons, a few small bells (to help sound an alarm), and bits of snowflake obsidian (for grounding). Sew the poppet shut.

Bless it to purpose by holding it in front of your Yule tree or gifts while repeating the following:

> Guarding now this sacred ground,
> keep our gifts quite safe and sound.

Hang the poppet guard in your tree or stash it among your gifts to keep them safe from harm or prying eyes. Ideally, place the poppet out of reach: it will appear to be an adorable Yule ornament, but you don't want others to touch or play with the poppet as this could dissipate the magick and affect its function.

Poppet

You can also create poppets of different shapes and styles for different functions. For example, a heart-shaped poppet could be stuffed with rose petals and saffron and attached to a sprig of mistletoe to encourage love, affection, and goodwill. Stuff a tree-shaped poppet with evergreen needles and juniper berries to bring the protective powers of the evergreen into a room. (It will smell good, too!) Hang this over your front door to safeguard those who enter or leave your home.

A Yule Log Talisman

The day after burning your Yule log, gather the cooled ashes. Sew them into a small magickal bag or poppet to create a talisman against lightning damage and house fires. Keep the talisman on your altar or use a tack to fasten it over an entrance door. On the next Yule, add the talisman to the kindling fire for that year's Yule log, sharing aloud your gratitude for the past year's well-being.

Spells to Bring Snow

Modern winter legends tell of workings and rituals guaranteed to bring snow, including:

- Wear pajamas backwards, brush your teeth with your opposite hand, flush at least six ice cubes down the toilet, and sleep with a silver spoon under the pillow. The backward pajamas supposedly confuse the "snow gods" (bonus points if the PJs have feet), flushing ice cubes is supposed to help create a "cold front," and the silver spoon tradition has an unknown origin but dates back hundreds of years.

- Toss ice cubes into a tree.
- Stack pennies on your windowsill. Each inch of pennies is supposed to equal an inch of snowfall.
- Place a white crayon in your freezer.
- Run around your table five times.

Sounds fun, yes? And they just might work—American schoolchildren (and teachers!) have sworn by these techniques for years.

An Appeal for Protection through Winter's Long Nights

As you prepare for bed, turn off all of the lights in your house but the one in your sleeping room. Light a candle if you wish, and repeat the following:

> *As we approach the year's longest night,*
> *I ask you, (insert deity or element),*
> *to be with me / and my loved ones*
> *and safeguard us through the hours.*
> *May we be blessed in community,*
> *bountiful in feast,*
> *and rich in the earth's gifts*
> *as we welcome the return of the light.*

As you finish, snuff the candle or turn off the single remaining light. For a variation, make this into your family's "good night" ritual by doing this together in a central location—such as the dining room or near the hearth—and then going silently to the bedrooms afterward.

Talisman for Protection During Travel

Fill a small magickal bag with small pieces of turquoise, tanzanite, and/or zircon (December birthstones with correspondences of power, protection, and calming). Add a few needles from an evergreen and, if available, a few dried hawthorn or juniper berries. Last but not least, add a bit of soil or a few pebbles from the threshold outside your front door—a bit of low magick crafts that keeps you connected to your home ground. Tie the bag shut with a strong cord. Tuck it into your car's glove box for safe travels during the winter holidays, or keep it with you during your travels.

A Talisman to Strengthen Family Connections

Select a number of holiday cards or gift tags received from friends and family. Shred or cut the cards and tags into small pieces; scent with a drop of juniper, cedar, or cinnamon oil; and use these to stuff a small cloth bag or poppet. If possible, add a small photograph of the loved one(s) to the bag. Tie shut and tuck this into your purse or briefcase; keep it with you to keep your loved ones close at heart—particularly if they are far from home.

Herbal Tea Magick

Make one or more of the following magickal blends:

- *Clear-seeing tea:* equal parts cinnamon and dried orange peel for mental clarity and psychic powers
- *Mind magicks tea:* two parts cinnamon and one part cardamom for intuition and psychic powers
- *Winter relaxer tea:* two parts spearmint and one part chamomile for rest and relaxation
- *Tummy-settling tea:* equal parts peppermint and thyme to ease stomach upset

To brew your infusion, place a heaping spoonful of mixture into an infuser in a warmed mug or teacup or just spoon the herbs directly into the cup. Fill with water that is very hot but not quite boiling; allow to steep for 3 to 5 minutes. Remove the infuser (or strain the mixture) and enjoy, swirling in a spoonful of honey if needed for sweetness. Use these teas as part of any magickal working—before, during, or after—or simply for a delicious moment during your winter day.

Variation: Spoon the herbs into a teacup (rather than a mug) and once the tea has steeped, drink without straining. Leave about a teaspoon of water in the cup, swirling it a few times, then read the tea leaves. (See page 99 for a quick discussion of tasseomancy.)

Generosity Charm

Save a favorite piece of ribbon from a favorite gift you've received, or, if that isn't possible, select an especially beautiful length of ribbon. Wrapping it around both hands, speak these words aloud:

> *However long*
> *the season be,*
> *my hands are working*
> *generously.*

Leave the ribbon on your altar throughout the holidays, and make a point of stopping daily to reflect on the spirit of generosity within your heart and home.

Variation: If the ribbon is long enough, bless it as above and use it to wrap a special gift for a loved one.

Magickal Winter Waters

Charged or energized waters—waters that have been exposed to specific elements, weather, celestial alignments, etc.—can be terrific additions to all sorts of spellcraft and ritual. The following are some ideas for making your own magickal waters:

- Fill a clean, clear glass jar with drinkable water. Expose the water to the Winter Solstice sunrise or moonrise or to other winter occasions that are important to you; leave the jar out for several hours.

- Waters charged under an eclipse are especially powerful.

- If possible where you live, collect dew on the solstice or during the winter.

- If it happens to rain or snow during the Winter Solstice, collect the rainwater or snow for later use.

- Collect rain or snow that falls during a severe winter storm.

- Break icicles, melt at room temperature, and save.

Use this water throughout the coming year for any number of purposes. For example:

- Use the water to anoint tools, charms, poppets, or other magickal items.

- Use it to dress candles or altar items.

- Sprinkle the water on plants or trees that need a magickal boost.

- Use it in ritual, whether as an offering, for water sharing or for the "ale" in cakes and ale.

- Use your charged waters to brew teas.

Variation: Save containers of snow or whole icicles in your freezer; use when spring arrives in a ritual designed to bid farewell to winter.

Blessing for Mothers

In the *Old Ways* chapter, we explored the idea of the sacred mothers of winter, and you may also want to think about honoring the divine feminine while setting up your seasonal altars or shrines. Many cultures and traditions recognize the female life force as the one that rebirths light and life back into the world at Midwinter.

Create a shrine for your favorite winter mothers—human or otherwise. Start with a base of white quilt batting (purchase this at your favorite fabric or craft store) and add a ring of short pieces of white yarn (for snow) and bits of straw. Sprinkle with glitter and set candles around the edges. In the center, place your favorite winter goddess figures, effigies, or photographs of magickal or human goddess figures. Use this altar as a focus for the darkness and rebirth inherent in the season, asking the mothers to bless your home in the year to come. When Midwinter has passed, tie some of the yarn and straw into a small bundle and save through the year on your regular altar. Or, save the yarn and straw to use for other magicks—they would make a fabulous stuffing for a dream pillow or poppet.

Make a "Porta-Pagan" Magick Set

One of the best parts of working magick is being able to work spontaneously, when the need or urge arises. But many Pagans aren't comfortable carrying magickal tools or supplies with them or having them visible to nonmagick folks. You can solve some of these problems and put magick in your hands with a Porta-Pagan magick set.

Start with an empty Altoids tin—or any similar tin used for small mints or candies. Leave it plain or decorate it with stickers, paint, or glued-on fabric. Then, line the inside in the same way. Tuck general materials useful for working magick inside. You can include tiny candles (hint: birthday cake candles can fit into plastic beads; the beads act as candle holders), a few strike anywhere matches, a small altar cloth, a packet of salt, a few gems or crystals (try quartz for general purposes; turquoise for protection and healing; and obsidian for grounding), a small vial of essential oils, an incense cone, a small mirror for scrying, or anything else that suits your purpose. Tuck this into a small bag, tied shut with a cord, and leave in your purse, briefcase, or glove box. You'll be ready for magick whenever the mood strikes.

Divination and Augury

Winter is a powerful and potent time for practicing divination (the use of tools and techniques to see into past, present, and future) and augury (the observing of naturally-occurring signs and omens). Whether we divine or augur, the process brings together magick, intention, intuition, and messages from the natural and magickal worlds to help us understand what's happening around us, what's happened in our past, and what's waiting around the next bend. We use divination to seek a deeper understanding of the world around us and of our place in it. We magickal types tend to be keen observers with heightened awareness and finely honed magickal antennae, and we long to make sense of the symbols, patterns, and hidden meanings that fill our daily lives. The quiet tone, long nights, darkness, themes of silence and rebirth, and crisp clarity of the air and heavens make winter a brilliant time for insights and inspirations.

What kinds of divination work well in winter? All of them! Whatever type of divination you like best will work especially well during winter's long, dark, crystalline nights, and it's also a great time to try something new. Have you had the urge to work more with tarot or to explore a new spread or even a new deck? Would you like to try your hand with the ogham, a pendulum, a Ouija board, runes, or a scrying crystal? Give it a try!

Just for fun, here are some specific ideas dedicated to the Winter Solstice.

Solstice Tree Tarot Spread

Shuffle and cut your tarot cards according to your usual procedures. For the Solstice Tree spread, lay the cards out from bottom to top and left to right.

- The trunk of the tree (card 1) is a signifier card, i.e., it's you or the person you're reading for.

- For the lower level of the tree, card 2 represents your ideas, card 3 your inspirations, and card 4 your plans.

- For the middle level, card 5 represents the process by which you will bring your plans to fruition, and card 6 shows any interventions or obstacles that might affect your progress (beneficial or otherwise).

- The tip of the tree (card 7) shows the final realization of your plans—the "gift" of your completion.

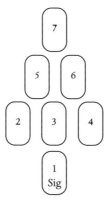

Tree Spread

Midwinter Solstice Tarot Spread

Place a signifier card and then place the three cards in an arc above it, working from left to right.

- Card 1 is you, the signifier. Imagine yourself deep within your winter cave.

- Card 2 is the card of contemplation. If winter is a time of reflection, evaluation, and contemplation, how is this affecting you? What are you thinking about?

- Card 3 is the card of celebration and action. Having reflected on the past year, how will you move forward? What's next?

- Card 4 is the card of light, realization, and success. As the sun reappears and light returns to the world, where will it find you?

Solstice Spread

Variations: In either spread, you may pull additional "more information" cards at any time. If there is a card you want to know more about, pull a new card and place it next to or above the original one. Examine the second card to see what it tells you about the first. Also, either spread may be adapted for work with runes.

Animal Track Omens

Depending on where you live, some animals visible during warm seasons won't be around much during the winter. On the other hand, if you live in a location with winter snow on the ground, you'll be able to easily spot tracks, which can make some animals more visible than they would be during warmer months. Use a field guide or online resources to identify the animal making the tracks, and consider what they're telling you. Is the animal crossing your path? Walking parallel with you? Watching you from a distance? Evaluate your discoveries and journal about them, adding a sketch or photograph of the omens.

Frozen Puddles and Frosted Panes

If you live in a snowy, icy clime, you can use icy surfaces (or even chunks of ice) for both scrying and divination. For divination, look for patterns, signs, or symbols in the frozen surface and consider what they might mean. For scrying, settle yourself in place and look deeply into the frozen surface, using it as you would use a crystal ball. Breathe slowly and evenly, and be prepared to scry for at least fifteen minutes and perhaps more, waiting to see what images or ideas appear to you. Record and journal about your results.

Winter Augury

Winter provides unique opportunities for this practice, which can include reading clouds, responding to patterns shown in fallen branches, watching December's Geminid meteor shower, observing patterns in flocks of birds, or even seeing shapes or intuiting meaning in snowbanks, to name only a few approaches. Good augury means using your imagination, staying alert, and finding time to be outdoors. Be aware of what is around you: looks for patterns or for anything unusual, such as an arrangement of feathers on the ground or an obvious image in the clouds overhead. You can also head out into nature and "ask" a specific question, waiting afterward to see if an answer is revealed. Once you have found something that speaks to you, evaluate your impressions and consider what they might mean. Again, I recommend journaling about your observations, and be sure to go back and review your notes later. Often, an augur seen on a specific day will come to have great meaning days or weeks later.

Weather Augury

A sub-category of augury is the idea of using weather signs to intuit the future. Here are a few examples:

- If the ice will bear a goose before Yule, it will not bear a duck after. (In other words, if the weather is cold and the ice thick before Midwinter, the weather will then be milder after.)

- If winter's first thunder is from the east, winter will soon be over.

- A windy Yule is said to bring good luck.

- A green Yule is believed to bring bad luck: snow or hard frost, in contrast, is considered a good omen. "A green Christmas makes a fat churchyard" (Danaher, 240).

A Few Folkloric and Customary Divinations

- Each person will receive one lucky month in the coming year for each holiday pudding sampled. (I wonder if this applies to eggnog, too?)

- The person who desires prophetic dreams should place nine mistletoe leaves in a handkerchief, tie it closed with nine knots, and sleep with it under the pillow.

- If one opens all the doors on midnight at Yule, evil and unkind spirits will depart.

- Persons born on Yule can see the little people.

- Eating a very large supper on New Year's Eve is believed to ensure plentiful food and wealth in the coming year.

- Put holly and ivy leaves under the pillow on New Year's Eve to dream of one's future husbands. Repeat this charm: "Oh ivy green and holly red, tell me, tell me, whom I shall wed."

- The Yule tree must be taken down by Twelfth Night or there will be bad luck.

- Withered holly and greenery should be burned to heat the pancake griddle.

It's fun to keep a record of your favorite augurs and folk sayings by writing them into your winter journal, and then see how many of them come true.

Tasseomancy

Tasseomancy is divination accomplished by reading tea leaves. To try it, you'll need loose tea or dried herbs and a teacup with a plain white interior. Place 1 teaspoon dried loose tea herbs into the teacup. Fill the cup with very hot (not boiling) water, top with a saucer, and steep for 5 minutes. Remove the saucer and enjoy the tea, leaving a bit of liquid in the bottom of the cup.

Now, pause and "ask" the tea leaves a silent question. Cover the teacup with your hand and swirl it deosil (sunwise) several times. Remove your hand and allow the marc—the wet leaf material—to settle. Observe it carefully. Are any shapes, patterns, or images clearly apparent, such as animals, trees, etc.? Does the marc create any impressions or insights? Have you received an answer to your question?

New Year's Divination and the Omen Days

The Welsh tradition of the Omen Days says that each day in Twelvetide corresponds to one of the months in the coming year. So December 25 corresponds with the following January, December 26 with February, etc. According to the lore, any omens, foreshadowings, predictions, or portents observed on the given date foretell what will transpire in the corresponding month. Do your own Omen Days forecast by carrying out your favorite divination on each day between December 25 and January 5. Write down your results so you can track them through the year.

A New Year's Divination Party!

Ask your magickal friends to join you on New Year's Eve with their favorite divination tools and favorite treats. Spend a couple of hours sharing techniques, then another hour or so giving and getting readings. Just before midnight, pour a libation for each person, turn off every light in the house, and gather around a single lighted candle. Together, repeat:

> *Gather we as old year ends*
> *together here with knowing friends*
> *as the New Year passes by*
> *open up our magick eyes.*

At the stroke of midnight, turn on the lights and have everyone do his or her own New Year's divination, remaining silent until everyone is finished. Then toast the New Year together, and celebrate!

Magick, altars, divination, the reading of signs are all wonderful ways to pass the winter hours, wouldn't you say? Have fun trying out these ideas and coming up with your own!

RECIPES
AND
CRAFTS

...compassion, wisdom, insight, search for meaning, sacrifice, ...

...tion and looking inward, evaluation, reflection, meditation, labo...

...on and scrying, study, journaling, tool crafting, feasting, comm...

...work, deep ritual, vigil personal retreat. Amaterasu, Baba...

...a, Bruno, Cailleach, Carlin, Carravogue, Ceres, Demeter, ...

...olda, Koliada, Lachesis, Marzana, Rind, Skadi, Snego...

Bacchus, Hodhr, Lugh, Saturn, Dewi Varsiloru, Cert, ...

...en Knight, Green Man, Holly King, Karkantzaros, Kn...

...Knitzelfrau, Pelznichol, Perchta, Samichlaus, Stallo, Th...

...mn, Egregores, green: evergreen, abundance, life, new beginning...

...wealth, gifts, prosperity, solar energy, red: holly berries and ...

...force, fire, white: silence, calm peace, protecting, cardamom: ...

...ticism, psychic powers, cinnamon: access to astral and spirit...

...tuition strength, cloves: attraction, authority, healing power, ...

...th, intuition, renewal, transformation, vitality, mistletoe: prote...

...st, protection, nutmeg, alertness, awareness, inspiration, intelle...

...t: calm, divination, intuition, psychic powers, relaxation, rosem...

...banishing, divination, healing, mental clarity, physical and p...

...a strength, sage: calm concentration, confidence, health and...

$\mathcal{W}$HETHER YOU CELEBRATE Yule, Christmas, Chanukah, or any of the many other winter holidays, recipes, decorations, and crafts are an important part of the event for most of us. Some of this goes back to the Pagan symbolism of the Winter Solstice and the use of lights, greenery, berries, wreaths, etc. Much of it is related to our desire to kindle warmth and light in the midst of winter. A lot of it, too, ties in with our desire to be with friends and family at a time of the year culturally linked with high celebration. And, of course, cooking, crafting, and decorating are an inexpensive and satisfying way to personalize the season—and they're just plain fun. In this chapter, we'll offer simple ideas for cooking and crafting your own holiday season.

Recipes to Enjoy at Home

The solstice has always been a time of joyful feasting in celebration of the return of light and life. When faced with the shortest day and longest night of the year, the ancients worried that sunlight would not return to nourish the land and banish the cold. It was this apprehension that led to the phrase "Eat, drink and be merry for tomorrow may never come." We still feel the same apprehension these days when, deep into winter, we're sure spring will never arrive. Feasting celebrates the return of bounty and focuses on celebration and gathering family together—and it can take on a decidedly magickal feel as well.

Many cultures have their own specific food traditions. For instance, in Sweden, an almond is stirred into the *julegrot* (Christmas pudding) and whoever finds the almond in their portion will have good luck throughout the coming year. When an English plum pudding is prepared, it's customary to have every family member take a turn with the stirring. Also in England, the traditional "bringing in the boar" may be reflected by a sturdy roast instead of entire suckling pig, but a roast—particularly a prime rib, crown roast of pork, or a roast turkey or goose—is still the centerpiece of many holiday tables.

There are many ways to add magick to your winter feast. Follow the custom of having every family member lend a hand in the "stirring," metaphorically speaking, mimicking the way each member of the community helps ensure the tribe's survival. Set a table with holiday colors and with your best dishes, goblets, and cutlery, and light plenty of candles. For a really special effect, have everyone gather at the table in a dark or semi-dark dining room. Recite a poem or blessing and light the candles, one by one, watching as everyone's faces are cast into the light. Offer toasts to family, departed ancestors, and guardian deities.

Sandy's Sugar Cookies

A wonderful, buttery, shortbread sugar cookie; the recipe makes 6–7 dozen cookies.

Ingredients:

1 cup sugar

1 cup powdered sugar

1 cup unsalted butter (not margarine!), softened

1 cup vegetable oil (not olive oil!)

2 eggs

1 teaspoon vanilla

1 teaspoon salt

1 teaspoon baking soda

1 teaspoon cream of tartar

4 ¾ cups all-purpose flour

Additional white sugar, for flattening; colored sugar, decors, and/or icing, as desired

Cream the sugar, powdered sugar, butter, and oil until light and fluffy. Add eggs and vanilla and mix well.

Add salt, baking soda, and cream of tartar and mix well. Add flour in increments, blending thoroughly after each addition. The dough will be light and somewhat sticky.

Drop dough by teaspoonfuls onto a cookie sheet. Flatten each ball slightly with the bottom of a glass dipped in white sugar.

If you want to use colored sugar or decors, sprinkle these on *before* baking.

Bake at 350°F until barely light brown on the edges, about 10 minutes. Don't overbake! Remove from cookie sheet immediately and cool on wire racks. If you want to frost and decorate the cookies further, wait until they're completely cool.

Ridiculously Rich Eggnog

Many of winter's traditional drinks reflect times past when alcohol was added to drinks as a preservative and spices were used to warm the stomach and conceal food spoilage. The best known of these libations is eggnog, an English-American creation sometimes known as flip-flip. Eggnog may have descended from posset, a hot British drink featuring eggs, milk, and either wine or ale. The word "nog" is British slang for strong ale. In the days before refrigeration, fresh milk spoiled quickly and thus wasn't part of the typical diet. Alcohol was often added to extend the shelf life of dairy and egg-based beverages.

Traditional eggnog features thickly beaten eggs combined with milk, heavy cream, and alcohol—usually brandy, bourbon, rum, or a combination. A generous grating of nutmeg is dusted over the creamy eggnog, which is topped with whipped cream and dipped up from a chilled glass bowl.

Ingredients:
3 eggs, separated (use fresh eggs from a trusted source)
6 tablespoons sugar
½ pint heavy cream (avoid "ultrapasteurized" varieties)
2 pints whole milk
¼ – ½ pint brandy, bourbon, and/or rum
½ tablespoon good-quality vanilla extract

Whole nutmeg

Additional heavy cream, whipped

In a big bowl, beat the egg yolks with 4 tablespoons of sugar until thick.

In a medium bowl, beat the egg whites with the remaining 2 tablespoons of sugar until thick.

In another medium bowl, beat the cream to soft peaks.

Add the cream to the yolks, fold in the egg whites, and add the milk, alcohol, vanilla, and a pinch of freshly grated nutmeg, if desired. Add magick by stirring deosil (sunwise). Pour the eggnog into a large bowl and chill in the freezer for about an hour before serving, until it turns a little icy.

To serve, pile more whipped heavy cream atop the bowl of 'nog and dust generously with more grated nutmeg. Spoon the eggnog into individual cups, and don't forget to toast!

Here We Come A' Wassailing!

Where eggnog may be the best-known winter drink of modern times, wassail is still the most traditional. The word *wassail* means "good health," and offered as a toast, with goblets raised, it implies drinking to vigor and wholeness. To go "a' wassailing" is to engage in seasonal revelry, usually with feasting, singing, and a good deal of alcohol. (Fools and misrules, anyone?)

In traditional terms, wassail is a traditional hot English beverage made by combining alcohol (particularly apple jack or apple brandy), fruit juices, and lots of winter spices: allspice, mace, nutmeg, cinnamon, and cloves. Whole small apples, oranges, and kumquats are often roasted and added to the mixture. In its traditional presentation, wassail is served from a large silver bowl and ladled into silver or pewter goblets with bright ribbons tied around their bases. In folk terms, wassail is also used as an apple tree spirit offering to bless orchards, drive away evil spirits, and increase their yields.

Custom also tells of Englishmen carrying a twelve-handled wassail bowl—made of applewood, of course—from house to house, where they would sing, drink, and have the bowl refilled before going on to the next house. It was a sign of good luck to have them visit.

Here's a wassail recipe that's friendly for all ages:

Ingredients:
2 quarts apple cider (hard cider or nonalcoholic)
3 cinnamon sticks
1 teaspoon whole allspice
½ teaspoon whole cloves
A grating of nutmeg
Several small apples
A couple of small mandarins or tangerines
A small handful of kumquats, raisins, and/or fresh cranberries (optional)
Plain or apple brandy (optional)

Put everything into a kettle and simmer gently until the apples' skins burst. Serve with a dollop of brandy for those who wish it. To simulate the ancient custom of apple wassailing, drink apple cider or wassail in an outdoor setting (under your fruit trees, if you have any), and offer a cheer to good fortune in the coming year. You might even take a mug or two to the neighbors.

Rumple Minze Pie

A variation on the well-known Grasshopper Pie, this pie uses Rumple Minze, a smooth peppermint schnapps. It's a perfect, light, and festive ending to a heavy holiday meal. The recipe makes 6–8 servings.

Crust ingredients:

Thin chocolate wafer cookies, crushed into fine crumbs (to yield 1¼ cups of crumbs)

5 tablespoons butter, melted

(Or, buy a ready-made chocolate cookie crust.)

Filling ingredients:

2/3 cup whole milk

30 large, fresh marshmallows

1 cup heavy cream

1 ounce crème de cacao (chocolate liqueur)

1 ounce Rumple Minze (peppermint schnapps)

Red food coloring (optional)

Crushed peppermints, fresh mint leaves, chocolate curls, and/or additional whipped cream (optional garnishes)

Preheat oven to 350°F. To make the crust: Combine crumbs and butter. Press into a 9 inch pie plate and bake for 10 minutes. Cool completely.

To make the filling: Heat the milk in a saucepan over low heat. When the milk is steamy, add the marshmallows and stir until dissolved and smooth. Cool to room temperature.

When the marshmallow mixture is cool, whip the cream. Gently fold the crème de cacao, Rumple Minze, and whipped cream into the marshmallow mixture. If desired, add 1–2 drops of food coloring to bake a soft-looking pale pink pie.

Pile the mixture into the cooled pie shell. Cover and freeze for 10–12 hours, or overnight.

To serve: Remove from freezer for about 10 minutes (for easier slicing). Garnish as desired, slice, and serve while still frozen.

Tree-Decorating Chili

This is the perfect meal to serve for tree-decorating night. It can be made ahead or can simmer while you decorate, and the leftovers are wonderful. For a meatless version, leave out the beef and add a second can of black beans. Serves 4 people.

Ingredients:
1 pound ground beef
1 onion, diced
8 ounces tomato sauce
15–16 ounces (1 can) stewed tomatoes
15–16 ounces (1 can) black beans, rinsed
8 ounces cooked pinto beans, rinsed
½ cup water
1 teaspoon salt
2 ½ teaspoons chili powder
¼ teaspoon cayenne pepper (add more later if desired)
Your choice of chili toppers: grated cheese, diced sweet
    onion, diced sweet pepper, sliced jalapeño, diced avocado,
    sour cream, corn chips

In a large frying pan or a 3–4 quart kettle, break up and brown the ground beef and onions. Spoon off and discard the fat.

Add the tomato sauce, stewed tomatoes, black and pinto beans, water, salt, chili powder, and cayenne. Bring to a gentle boil and then lower to a simmer. Simmer for about 2 hours, uncovered. If it becomes thicker than you'd like, add a bit more water as needed.

Before serving, check and adjust salt and pepper as needed. Serve the chili in a bowl and customize with your choice of toppers.

Variations: Ladle the chili over a hot dog in a sturdy bun for delicious chili dogs. The chili is also wonderful spooned into a steaming hot baked potato or (weird but true) spooned over corn chips.

Foil Dinners

Children love cooking foil dinners in the fireplace, but you can also make these in the oven if you don't have a hearth. Serves 4 people.

Ingredients:
1–1½ pounds raw ground meat (beef is preferred), crumbled
4 medium potatoes, peeled and cubed
1–2 thinly sliced onions
4 carrots, sliced
2 cans cream of mushroom soup
1 cup water
Salt and pepper
Heavy-duty aluminum foil

If using the fireplace, start by building a fire and letting it burn down to a thick bed of coals—this will take about an hour. If using the oven, preheat to 400°F.

For each person, lay out a double-thick 18" square of foil. Each person builds his or her own foil dinner, adding everything but the water.

Place the food on the double-thickness of foil and fold both layers of foil carefully around the food, enclosing it entirely and sealing the packet completely (a "drugstore seal" is recommended) so the juices can't leak out. Just before closing the foil, carefully add the water. This is an important step as the water will turn into steam during cooking, helping cook the food thoroughly and avoiding burning. Seal the packet completely, leaving a small amount of air space.

Place the packets on the hot coals (or place on a cookie sheet in the oven). Cook for 30–40 minutes, turning a couple of times. Don't poke holes in the foil!

When you hear sizzling and begin smelling the cooking meat, wait about five more minutes, then open one packet as a test. Careful: there will be hot steam inside. If the dinner is not quite done, rewrap and return to the coals for a bit longer.

Variations: Just about any combination of meats and/or veggies will work, and different soups can be used, too. Vegetarians and vegans can omit the meat and soup as needed.

A Grown-Up Treat: The Yuletini

Four to six weeks before you wish to celebrate, make **Cranberry Cordial:**

In a 1-quart Mason jar, combine 1 cup sugar and 2 cups finely chopped fresh cranberries. Fill the jar with a good-quality vodka (you'll need about 1 cup). Cap this and allow it to sit on the kitchen counter for 3 to 4 weeks, shaking it once or twice daily. After 3 to 4 weeks, strain it into a clean jar and store in the refrigerator. It makes a brilliant red, sweet-tart cordial that is wonderful as an apéritif. It's also a terrific gift, given in a decorative beribboned jar.

But, even better, keep it yourself and make a Yuletini!

Ingredients for one Yuletini:

½ tablespoon whole berry cranberry sauce (homemade is best!)

Juice from half of a large Satsuma or Clementine mandarin (plus some of the peel)

3 tablespoons cranberry cordial

Ice

Chill a martini glass with ice. Empty the ice; place the cranberry sauce in the glass and muddle to break up the berries. Combine the juice, cordial, and ice in a small shaker and shake until mixed and chilled. Strain the mixture into the martini glass; garnish with orange peel. Yum! (For a mocktail, use 1 tablespoon cranberry sauce, add the mandarin juice, and top off with your favorite sparkling beverage.)

Recipes for Gifting and Sharing

The winter holiday season is well known as a time for parties and a steady stream of treats. Here are a few of my holiday favorites, perfect for you and your family and also for giving and sharing at get-togethers.

Soup Herbs and the Bouquet Garni

A gift of soup is welcomed by just about everyone, and good soup always begins with good herbs. The bouquet garni, literally a "garnished bouquet," is a small bundle of herbs used to flavor stock, soups, and stews as well as braises and pot roast.

You will need:

Cheesecloth, cut in 9 inch circles (nine being a very magickal number)

Assorted dried aromatic soup herbs: rosemary, thyme, chervil, whole allspice, peppercorns, dried garlic slivers, parsley, and celery seed

Natural string (cotton or hemp), cut in 9 inch lengths

Half-pint Mason jars with lids

Heavy paper

Pen or permanent marker

Lay out circles of cheesecloth, with three layers in each pile. Place the various dried herbs on the circles, choosing freely from the above list. Gather the circles up into a hobo-style packet and tie shut with the string, leaving some string for removing the bag from the pot.

Collect the bundles or bouquets in a glass jar for gifting—you will be able to get four to six garnis into a jar, depending on how full you stuff them.

Add a label that lists the ingredients and instructions: "Drop one bundle into a kettle of soup or stock, and simmer as long as needed. Remove and discard the bundle before serving. Store the jar of unused bundles in a cool, dry place."

A Hot Chocolate Kit

The word "chocolate" comes from the Mayans, one of the earliest-known users of cacao-based drinks both as a daily beverage and in religious ceremonies. Their chocolate drinks featured chili peppers, creating a drink that was hot in more ways than one. Dark chocolate has been found to be rich in antioxidant chemicals, which repair cell damage and slow aging. The easiest way to make hot chocolate is to melt high-quality chocolate into milk, adding sweeteners and herbs or spices as desired.

You will need: (Makes two gifts)
12 ounces dark chocolate chips
1 teaspoon dried red pepper flakes *or* ½ teaspoon cayenne pepper
2 teaspoons raw turbinado sugar
Wax paper
Baking sheet
2 half-pint Mason jars with lids
Heavy paper
Pen or permanent marker
2 small (4 inch) wire whisks (optional)

In a microwave-proof glass bowl, microwave the chocolate chips just until they soften slightly. Stir in the red pepper flakes or cayenne pepper and the sugar and mix well. Spoon the chocolate mixture into a wax paper-lined baking sheet and allow to cool until brittle.

Chop the chocolate mixture into small pieces and use to fill the jars. Label with instructions: "Add a heaping spoonful of chocolate chunks to a cup of steaming hot milk. Stir until the chocolate melts, whisking to blend." If you like, tie a small whisk to each jar.

Mulling Spices

Mulling is an ancient process in which spices and herbs are infused into hot cider, juice, or spirits to make a delicious drink. Giving a gift of mulling spices will bring this treat into your loved ones' kitchens.

You will need: (Makes two gifts)
Cheesecloth, cut in 9 inch circles
About a cup of assorted whole spices: broken cinnamon
    sticks, allspice berries, star anise, whole cardamom, pep-
    percorns, chunks of dried vanilla bean, and/or cloves
Several strips of dried citrus peel (prepare this by stripping
    peel from oranges or lemons several days earlier)
Whole nutmeg
Natural string (cotton or hemp), cut in 9 inch lengths
2 half-pint Mason jars
Heavy paper
Pen or permanent marker

Lay out circles of cheesecloth, with three layers in each pile. Place an assortment (2–4 tablespoons) of whole spices and citrus peels on the cheesecloth. Grate fresh nutmeg onto the mixture, and tie the packet into a small bundle. Pack the small bundles into the Mason jar—each jar should hold about six bundles, depending one how full you stuff them.

Label with these instructions: "Add one bundle to one quart apple cider or red wine. Simmer over medium heat for about an hour. Sweeten with brown sugar to taste and, if desired, add a dollop of brandy. Enjoy!"

As an option, you may also simply fill a glass jar with a mixture of finely chopped spices and citrus peels. Instruct the user to add 1 tablespoon of the mixture to 8 ounces of very hot cider or red wine, allow the mixture to infuse for 15–30 minutes, and strain before drinking.

Bath Salts

Everyone can use a little pampering at the solstice, and your friends will love this gift.

You will need: (Number of gifts varies)
Table or dendritic salt
Essential oil (lavender, mint, rosemary, juniper, and chamomile are good options)
Coarse-grained Kosher salt (or a deeply colored artisanal salt, such as Hawaiian black salt or Himalayan pink salt)
Epsom salt
Coarse or extra-large grained sea salt
Wide-mouthed glass pint jar with a lid for *each* gift
¼ cup measuring cup
Heavy paper
Pen or permanent marker

Place the table (or dendritic) salt into a small bowl. Scent the salt with several drops of essential oil and stir well.

Place enough of the scented salt into a jar to fill it about one fourth of the way. Add, in layers, ¼ cup scoops of the other salts. Top with a final layer of the remaining scented table salt, adding a few more drops of essential oil. The different salts have different textures and slightly different colors, and the visible layers will show through the glass and look gorgeous.

Screw on the lid, and use a ribbon to attach the label to the jar. Label with these instructions: "To use, add a ¼ cup scoop of salts into a hot bath. Scoop deeply so you get some of each salt in the bath, or stir or shake the jar before using. Relax! Ahhhh…"

Mason Jar Crafts: Bath Salts (top), Bouquet Garni (left),
Hot Chocolate Kit (right)

Crafting and Decorating the Home

Setting the mood and making your home warm and inviting will make the winter months more fun, more comfortable, and more magickal. Plus, making seasonal changes in your home decor is a way to help you "bond" with the holiday season. These don't have to be complicated changes: put soft flannel sheets on the bed and add seasonal towels, quilts, and table linens around your home. Splashes of red, green, and gold evoke the season and add to the festivity and celebration.

If you have a fireplace, bring in a small stack of firewood and perhaps buy or make some of those amazingly cinnamon-scented pinecones. No fireplace? No problem! Set out candles scented with bayberry, cinnamon, or evergreen—for extra safety, nestle them into tall Mason jars before lighting and set them atop a mirror for extra brilliance. Toss warm lap quilts or throws over your couches or chairs, ready for friends and family to enjoy.

Perfume your home by simmering cinnamon sticks, whole cloves, and strips of orange peel in a pan of water on the stove —your very own version of holiday incense. Put the kettle over very low heat, and keep a close eye on it, adding water as needed to keep it from going dry. Not only will your home smell wonderful, but this also has a healthful humidifying action, helping to moisturize the often too-dry winter air that fills our homes during the cold months.

Altars and Shrines

Creating a seasonal solstice shrine or altar will help you sync with the season and feel its beauty, and creating a seasonal altar space is just plain fun. You might choose to arrange it via your traditional altar arrangement, including your usual magickal tools, seasonal deity figures, and the like, perhaps starting with an altar cloth of red, green, or gold and then adding white or gold candles, small lights, and whatever else is part of your usual setup. Placing a mirror atop the altar cloth and then placing your items on the mirror will add wonderfully to the sensation of brilliance and light.

You could also create your altar as a winter tableau, using a base of white quilt batting as "snow" and arranging tiny lighted ceramic houses, animal figurines, trees, and other wintery additions. Small mirrors make excellent frozen ponds, and glitter and bits of silver or gold garland add shininess. Surround the altar with lots of tiny white lights or use candles of red, green, gold, silver, white, or bayberry. Add figures to represent the Green Guest, Santa, or deity figures of your choice. This sort of altar has an added benefit in that it can be displayed "in plain sight" and works both as a sacred space and as part of your Midwinter decor.

Why stop with one shrine? Midwinter is a time for celebration and decoration, and this can be reflected with multiple altar spaces in multiple rooms. During Yuletide, you might have several: for instance, a couple of altars in the living area, one in the bedroom, and one on the kitchen windowsill—all adorned with lights and baubles. Use your winter shrines as a focus for daily meditation, contemplation, and magickal workings as you prepare to greet the coming of Yule.

Let There Be Light!

Lights emphasize the returning warmth of the Winter Solstice sun, and you really can't have too many lights at Midwinter. Buy extra strings of lights and use them in every room. They'll return light back to your little corner of the world, add energy to your rooms, and lift the mood of everyone who sees them. Watch for Yule decorations to start hitting the stores somewhere between mid-August and Samhain; shop early for the best variety, and then shop late in December to snap up last-minute sales and bargains.

Luminarias

A beautiful source of traditional light, luminarias are made by placing a few inches of sand in a paper bag and anchoring a lit votive candle in the sand; the lit candle glows through the bag, providing a diffuse, golden light. To make a winter luminaria, place a votive candle into a glass Mason jar, allowing the candlelight to illuminate the surrounding snow and ice. For an even niftier effect, stack chunks of ice (or snowballs) around the luminaria jar, igloo-style, leaving the mouth of the jar open so you can light the candle. Once lit, the luminaria will glow bluish-white (ice and snow absorb light from the red end of the visible spectrum but leave the blue end untouched, causing the blue appearance). Use luminarias to define an outdoor ritual space, or line them up to highlight a path or adorn the front of your home.

Greenery

Second only to the Winter Solstice symbol of light comes the tradition of winter greenery. It has long been traditional to bring evergreens into one's home at winter, especially around the time of the solstice. Evergreens were cherished at this time of year as natural symbols of rebirth and resurrection amid winter's symbolic deathly sleep. Since evergreens remain green throughout the winter, they have long appeared in Yule celebrations as symbols of the still-living world. The holiday trees, wreaths, and garlands that people still hang today go back to these traditions.

The magickal correspondences of evergreens, as a group, include continuity of life, protection, and prosperity—important qualities when one considers the dangers of winter. Holly and ivy are both known for protection and luck. Holly is ideal for decorating doors, windows, and fireplaces because of its prickliness: it can ward off or snag and capture evil spirits before they enter and harm the household: sort of like flypaper for faeries.

Another familiar holiday green is mistletoe, a plant that is both poisonous and parasitic. Folk names for mistletoe include all-healing, sap of the oak, and Druid's weed. Mistletoe is believed to have been sacred to the Druids and is often found growing in oak trees, which was also important to the Druids and ancient Celts. Legend says that Celtic Druids used golden sickles to cut mistletoe, ideally on the sixth night after the full moon before either solstice. White linen would be stretched out under the trees to catch the falling mistletoe and prevent it from touching the ground, for if the mistletoe touched the ground, all of the plant's sacred energy would pour back into the earth.

Believed to be a magickal aphrodisiac, bunches of mistletoe are hung over doorways today to bring luck and fertility. Mistletoe is also an effective protective plant: hang a sprig of mistletoe over a major doorway or threshold and leave it there until the next Yule as a charm for good luck and protection. Or, if you prefer, take it down at Midsummer and sacrifice it to the Midsummer bonfire.

Wreaths and garlands—made from evergreens and decorated with berries, seeds, cones, and ribbons—are another way to work with holiday greenery. The circular shape of a wreath easily symbolizes the Wheel of the Year and the returning sun. As for garlands, they may not be round, but they certainly add to the celebratory festivity.

The Solstice Tree

We can't talk about Midwinter without talking about having a solstice tree. As discussed previously, it has long been a tradition to bring greenery into the home at Midwinter, and a decorated tree was part of this. The Pagan Midwinter tree eventually inspired Christian traditions. According to John Matthews, "The first historically recorded mention of Christmas trees actually comes from an anonymous German citizen. … Writing in 1605 he comments, 'At Christmas they set up fir trees in the parlours of Strasbourg and hang thereon roses cut out of many colored paper, apples, wafers, gold-foil, sweets, etc.'"

Many cultures and societies have tree-decorating traditions. Greek farmers once brought their landholders a *rhamna* on Christmas morning. The *rhamna* was a pole festooned with wreaths of myrtle, rosemary, olive, and bay leaves and decorated with flowers and metallic papers. In Circassia, a young pear tree was selected to be laden with candles and topped with a cheese. (Yes, a cheese!) The tree was carried door-to-door throughout the Solstice night (Matthews, 82). This was said to bring luck and good tidings, especially when wine was shared at each threshold.

In eighteenth-century England and Germany, the traditional Christmas tree was often replaced with a pyramid of wood and dowels, decorated with ribbons, papers, and evergreen boughs so as to imitate a conical fir tree. The spaces in the "branches" were filled with fruit and nuts. After being carried throughout the home, the pyramid was settled in the main living room or parlor, and it became the focus of the holiday celebrations. Today, this tradition is continued with wooden candle towers—the ones that hold lit candles and spin as the heat from the candles rises and pushes a number of wooden paddles. Most of these are tabletop versions, but some are building-high!

Crafts for Gifting and Sharing

Gift giving is a tradition long associated with the Winter Solstice and other winter holidays. It's an act of loving kindness, and gifts are even better when they've been selected thoughtfully or when you've made them yourself, for this infuses them with your love, vitality, and magickal creativity.

Take time to wrap and beribbon your gifts so they shine with color and light. You might use the Swedish custom of writing half-poems or clues on the gift tag that hint at what's within. A magickal friend of mine creates gift tags that are also magickal talismans, ready to be plucked off the package and carried for prosperity, protection, or success.

Let's look at some fun project ideas.

Making Candles

Making candles isn't difficult and is lots of fun. Here are some ideas:

- *Rolled beeswax candles* are simple to make. Place a length of wick on a sheet of soft beeswax and then roll the wax up in a tight cylinder, creating a taper with the wick protruding. These candles look rustically pretty and smell great; however, they're soft and burn quickly.

- *Dipped candles* are another approach. Melt paraffin in a double boiler (or in a clean can set in a pan of hot water) over low heat. Tie a length of wick (the wick should be as long as your finished candle) to a pencil and dip it into the paraffin, raising the pencil to allow the waxed wick to cool and harden. Repeat this over and over, allowing the wick to accumulate a growing layer of wax. The more times you dip, the thicker your candle will become. When finished, allow the candle to cool for 24 hours by suspending the pencil over two jars. Trim the wick and use.

- *Molded candles* can be fun to make. Select a candle mold (small waxed dairy cartons and small cans work well) and coat the inside with a thin later of vegetable oil. Tie a length of wick to a pencil and set it atop the mold, with the wick hanging down into the mold. Fill the mold with melted paraffin. Allow to cool for 24 hours and then remove the mold. Wipe off any residual oil and use.

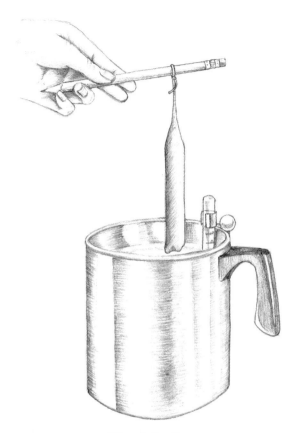

Dipped Candles

- *Ice candles*—fun to do and so appropriate for winter! Suspend a candlewick over a clean waxed carton (e.g., a milk carton) or a candle mold, then fill completely (for best results, overfill just a little) with small ice cubes (¾–1 inch ice is an ideal size). Return to the freezer for thirty minutes so container and ice are completely chilled. Remove from the freezer and quickly pour in melted paraffin, pouring from different positions so the entire candle is filled. The ice will melt and the wax will harden quickly, leaving spaces where the ice was. Allow the candle to cool for about an hour, then—working over the sink—remove the candle from the mold, allowing water to drain off. Let dry for a day before using.

Ice Candles (Finished Product)

With any of these candle options, you can use bits of broken crayon to add color to your melted paraffin. You can also add crystal chips, herbs, essential oils, or small items to your candles before or during the pouring/rolling process. If using the finished candles in specific workings or ritual, you might "dress" them with an appropriate essential oil. Dip your fingertip in the essential oil and anoint the candle, tracing from bottom to top of the candle for workings involving growth, beginnings, or expansion and from top to bottom for diminishings or endings.

Caution! Use low heat when melting paraffin, and watch it closely. If it gets too hot, it can spontaneously burst into flame.

The Great Christmas Candle

Some Celtic traditions use a one-week candle called *coinneal mór na Nollaig*, the "Great Christmas Candle," which is lit throughout the season and particularly on Christmas Eve (Freeman). The candle is associated with goodwill and fair fortune. You can follow this tradition with a store-bought candle or make your own, encompassing a span of days important to you, your family, or your own magickal traditions.

The traditional candle is red, but any color may be used. For extra safety, stand the candle inside a tall Mason jar. As the candle is lit, repeat the following: *The Great Christmas Candle is lit on this night, may goodwill and fair fortune follow us through the New Year.* Turn this into a family or group ritual by allowing family members to light their own small candles from the larger ones. Turn it into a holiday gift by presenting a friend with his own Great Christmas Candle nestled in a bed of greenery and with instructions attached.

Making an Evergreen Wreath

It's easy to make a wreath for your front door. Buy a wire form at a florist shop or craft store. Into it, insert evergreen and holly sprigs, berries, dried seed heads, grasses, or anything else that reflects your local area during the winter—you might even wander through your yard or neighborhood to see what pieces of dried wonders would make beautiful additions. Adorn the finished wreath with red or gold ribbons, small ornaments, or whatever suits your personal or magickal purposes.

Leaves of Gratitude: A Solstice Tree Craft

Cut leaf shapes from green and gold construction paper. Have your family members use colored, metallic, or glitter pens to write expressions of gratitude on each leaf. You might also use the leaves for inscribing wishes or magickal charms. Tie these into your Yule tree or wreath or thread them into garlands; they'll be concrete expressions of your gratitude and wishes for the past year. When the season is over, collect and burn the leaves as part of a final fire, saying goodbye to Yule until the next year.

A Gift for the Birds: A Solstice Tree Craft

When it's time to take down the tree, consider making it into a gift for the birds—a great project for your favorite youngsters. String blueberries, cranberries, and popcorn on cotton string (or dental floss) and hang from the limbs. Shelled, unsalted peanuts; unsweetened oat cereal (such as regular Cheerios); and chunks of orange, apple, and pear can also be strung and will be much appreciated by the birds. Fill orange or satsuma halves with mixtures of peanut butter and sunflower seeds. Small pinecones or fir cones can also be stuffed with peanut butter, nuts, and seeds. You can visit the local feed store for suet cakes and dried sunflower heads: affix these to the tree with twine. Don't forget to put out a saucer of water and change it daily. Fresh water sources are prized by winter birds and will attract them to your yard almost as effectively as the food will. Place your "bird tree" where you'll be able to watch it easily, and prepare to be entertained!

PRAYERS
AND
INVOCATIONS

...mission, wisdom, insight, search for meaning, sacrifice, eternity,
...nd looking inward, evaluation, reflection, meditation, hibernation
...d scrying, study, journaling, tool crafting, feasting, communal
..., deep ritual, sigil personal retreat, Amaterasu, Baba Yaga
...rune, Cailleach, Carlin, Carravogue, Ceres, Demeter, Decima,
...Koliada, Lachesis, Marzana, Rind Skadi, Snegurochka,
...hus, Hodhr, Lugh, Saturn, Dilis Varsvlavu, Cert, Elves,
...night, Green Man, Holly King, Karkantzaros, Knecht
...tzelfrau, Pelznichol, Perchta, Samichlaus, Stallo, Tomten,
Egregores, green: evergreen, abundance, life, new beginnings, wea
...th, gifts, prosperity, solar energy, red: holly berries and poinse
...fire, white: silence, calm peace, protecting, cardamom: divinat
..., psychic powers, cinnamon: access to astral and spiritual re
...v strength, cloves: attraction, authority, healing power, protec
...tution, renewal, transformation, vitality, mistletoe: peace, pros
...rotection, nutmeg, alertness, awareness, inspiration, intelligence,
...lm, divination, intuition, psychic powers, relaxation, rosemary:
...hing, divination, healing, mental clarity, physical and psychic
...ength, sage: calm concentration, confidence, health and healing

$\mathcal{L}$ONG BEFORE "MODERN" humans even thought about creating a modern calendar, they were ruled by the turning of the seasonal wheel. In the spring, the land came to life and positively hummed with new energies and beginnings. In summer, the world sang aloud with fertile energy and a sense of fecund, green plenty. In autumn, the song became quieter; the land went fallow, and efforts were turned toward bringing in crops against the long, hard winter. And then winter came, and the land fell silent during the long, cold, dark months.

These seasonal changes also work as a metaphor for the human soul. In spring, the soul feels the push of life, the motivation to reach outward, experimenting with newborn ideas and experiences. In summer, with life in full swing, the soul rejoices in the pure, open gifts of the growing world. In autumn, the soul begins to withdraw, becoming introspective as it prepares to meet the winter. And in that winter, the soul quiets and draws inward, seeking an essential core of meaning.

Ancient cultures inevitably developed rounds of prayers, meditations, and invocations to take them through these stages of life. Winter was always a key time for such events, for winter—a time when the land falls silent and appears to sleep—is a time when the world of spirits and insights seems not only closer than at other times but also feels more necessary. As we gird our souls against winter's darkness and await the return of the light, we have a powerful opportunity to look inward and contemplate our relationship to nature, magick, those we love, and those whose need is greater than ours. We also can deepen our relationships with the spiritual and with ourselves.

The following prayers, invocations, meditations, and other ideas are meant to be used for rituals, spellwork, or any sort of magickal workings. None of these are aimed at inviting the deity to take over and "ride" one's body; some are focused on appealing to or entreating a deity to join us in the sacred space, while others encourage us to turn inward and still others honor the winter season itself and the return of the life-giving sun.

At those times when we feel anxious, it's not unusual for people to turn to prayer. To pray is to make a solemn appeal or request for assistance from a deity figure, energy source, or religious object. I've heard many people say, "But Pagans don't pray." I disagree. If you're talking to our gods, appealing to them, and asking for guidance or assistance, you're praying. The root of the word *pray* derives from the Latin "to obtain by entreaty," and that's exactly what we do in ritual and in much

PRAYERS AND INVOCATIONS

spellwork. A prayer is a personal conversation between you and your gods.

As for invocation, the word means "to call" and refers to summoning (invoking) a deity, elemental power, or other supernormal being. Making suggestions on the how-tos of invocation is beyond the scope of this book, but here are two sound pieces of advice. First, when working with deities, it's best to *invite* them—most of them don't take kindly to being bossed around. Second, never (!) invoke what you don't know how to banish.

Structure for a Simple Prayer

Follow this four-part guideline to create your own prayers:

1. Welcome and acknowledgement: speak the deity's name and acknowledge their qualities and gifts.

2. Gratitude: express thanks for gifts and support the deity has already given you.

3. Intercession or request: make your appeal or request.

4. Thankful release: express gratitude for the deity's attention and grace.

Note: some people make offerings as part of their prayer; if you'd like to do this, insert them at what seems like the most opportune point.

Here is a sample prayer:

[Welcome] Goddess Holda, bringer of prosperity and fertility, I pray to you on this winter evening. [Gratitude] I am grateful for the care with which you've watched over my family in the last year, for we have been strong and healthy. [Request] I beseech you to once again watch by us in the year to come, insuring our well-being and good fortune. [Release] Thank you for your gifts, Divine Mother. I remain your devout servant. May you know peace.

Invocation to the Old Woman of Winter

This would work for most female winter deities as well.

Ancient mother of Midwinter,
watcher over life and death,
the one who rebirths the world,
be with us on this longest night!
See us through the dark hours
and stand with us
as dawn births the promise of new life.
So mote it be!

Invocation to Father Yule

This would work for most male winter deities as well.

Heroic father, giver of life,
one who stands with sword in hand
to fight against the dangers of the wild,
bring that sword into our circle
and stand with us against this night's darkness.
For the night is long,
and you will keep us safe.

Invocation to the Life-Giving Sun on the Solstice Vigil

Oh, absent sun,
the earth grows cold as we wait.
Our vigil fire is but a small spark
compared to your brilliance.
Our bones grow cold
awaiting your warmth.
Patiently we await your return
in the eastern sky.
Impatiently we await the first shard of light
piercing the eastern dawn—
the first sign of life's renewal.

Come to us, oh sun!
For now, we wait.

Meditation: An Introduction

With autumn comes a cooling of temperatures and a slow ebbing of daylight. Our bodies respond to these changes with decreased energy levels and sometimes changes in our overall resistance or stamina, and these changes continue as we move into winter. During the holiday season, we tend to spend a lot of time thinking about other people and perhaps not so much thinking about ourselves. Combined with the fact that many of us spend most of the fall and winter indoors, it's no surprise that we may feel rundown and develop illnesses during the dark months.

Some of the factors that keep us healthy include a varied diet, a proper amount of sleep, and regular exercise, all of which should be maintained through the winter. Minimizing stress is also extra important, particularly given the craziness of the December holiday season. Many experts recommend meditation as a valuable way to increase relaxation and enhance immunity. Meditating for even five to ten minutes a day is known to relieve stress, promote a sense of calm, and support the immune system and overall health.

Before we begin, here are a couple of practical suggestions. Most meditations presented in person start with the instruction to "close your eyes," the purpose being to remove visual input and thus reduce distraction. Unfortunately, for people who are hard of hearing, closing their eyes means they cannot see the speaker and cannot follow along. Similar problems occur with recorded meditations: if a hard-of-hearing person cannot see the words, she can't follow along. Likewise, a person who is visually impaired can't see printed words and must hear the spoken guidelines in order to participate. Make whatever adjustments are needed to make meditation work for you. Close your eyes or open them. Read the words from a paper or listen to them. Some folks record the meditation into a smart phone recorder and then listen to the playback. Do what works for you.

A Simple Winter Breathing Meditation

Sit in a chair in a quiet room at a time when you will not be disturbed. Pick a time of day when you are not fatigued—morning works well.

Close your eyes and breathe in and out, slowly and regularly.

Imagine a glow of light just below your navel. With each breath you take, it grows bigger.

Continue to breathe and glow until you feel that your entire body is surrounded in soft, glowing light. Be aware of this light and how it moves with your breathing and heartbeat. Maintain this for as long as you're able—at least ten minutes.

When you're ready to finish, lift your arms slowly overhead and exhale powerfully, as if blowing out a giant candle.

Lower your arms slowly, and feel the glow fade away until it disappears. Or, you may wish to keep a little bit of it with you through the day.

A Winter Meditation

While most meditations tend to mellow us out, this one is decidedly aimed at energizing. I recommend doing it in the morning; do it at night and you may have trouble sleeping.

Settle yourself in a quiet room at a time in which you will be undisturbed. Wear loose clothing and sit in a way that feels comfortable. Lay your hands quietly in your lap with your fingers relaxed. Follow this meditation, breathing slowly and with intention:

> You are sitting on a log in a forest clearing. The log is rough and cold. The air is cold, maybe freezing. As you breathe, in and out, you feel the cold air pull deep inside of you. You feel bits of snow falling gently against your skin. Everything is silent around you. You are silent, too. Your mind is silent. Your breathing is silent. Your thoughts are silent. You feel yourself as one with the winter night. A deep peacefulness comes over you. You sit quietly for some time, feeling this peaceful quiet.

(Allow some time to pass.)

Still enfolded in silence, you become aware of a sensation deep within you. It is the smallest hint of warmth, as if a candle was flickering deep inside. You focus on the warmth; it isn't yet enough to create actual heat, but it is real. As you wait, the warmth begins to grow steadily. You imagine a tiny ball of warmth and light inside you. Now it's about the size of a walnut. Now it's the size of a small orange. Now a grapefruit. You feel it hum—it feels alive. It feels wonderful. It fills you with warmth, and you sit with it, basking in how good it feels. You feel warm and completely safe.

You become aware of the log you're sitting on, which no longer feels rough and cold but now feels warm and inviting. The air around you feels warmer, too. The air you pull in and out, in and out of your lungs is gently warm and feels moist. Without looking, you become aware that there are other logs around you, and that others sit on the logs, just as you sit on yours. Without looking you know that these are your loved ones. You can see each of their faces. You smile, then you pull back to focus again on long, slow, warm breaths. You become aware that all of the logs are arranged in a circle around a great fire pit. A huge pile of wood is arranged in the pit; the pile is dark and silent.

As you keep breathing silently, in and out, you become aware of a small bit of light in the center of the woodpile. It's as if the small flame that once burned within you has now found its way into the wood. As you breathe in and out, it's as if your breath feeds the flame. When you breathe in, the tiny flame rises up, a little higher each time. When you breathe out, the flame pushes away momentarily and then rushes up again. In and out, in and out.

The flame begins to grow. You can hear the wood hissing and crackling as it catches fire. The fire grows. Soon, the fire pit is alive with light and sound. Your breathing picks up slightly from the excitement. You can feel the heat coming from the fire—it warms your face and makes you feel alive. You reach your hands out toward the flame and imagine the warmth filling you with life and energy. You're aware of your loved ones doing the same. Together with them, a circle of energy surrounds the bonfire and courses through you. You have never felt more alive! Your heart and soul sing with energy.

As you experience this, as you feel the light and energy and joy, the scene is suddenly rent by a shard of light from the rising solstice sun, and even the fire cannot compete with the sun's brilliance. Holding this scene in your mind's eye, you take three slow, deep, breaths before opening your eyes.

Go forth into your day, energized and inspired!

The Holy Midwinter Nights Meditation

The word "holy" means "whole," and this meditation helps us search for wholeness of spirit and soul and contemplate our relationships with self, other beings, and the universe. The meditation is inspired by works done by Carl Jung, Rudolph Steiner, and Joseph Campbell. The following demonstrates one night's worth of meditation and then gives you a list of topics to develop for additional nights.

- A focus aspect (theme)
- An opening reading
- A focus activity
- A moment of gratitude or thankfulness
- A closing reading
- A reflective process afterward
- An intentional carrying forward of the meditation into the next day

Select a quiet, private place to do this meditation. Ideally, it should be done in the evening just before bed. Create a quiet, peaceful atmosphere with gentle lighting—candles or firelights are ideal. Sit quietly, aware of your breathing, and focus on a candle flame or a selected focal point.

Night 1: Soul Touch

Props: Pictures of loved ones, important pieces of personal memorabilia.

Opening reading: "Happiness resides not in possessions, and not in gold. Happiness dwells in the soul." —Democritus

Focus activity: Where is your beginning? Where do you come from? Let your mind flow back in memory to your earliest recollections. Slip into a meditative mode that takes you deep into primordial oceans or out into the universe of primordial "star stuff," the atoms of creation. Where was your soul born? Where will it go next?

Gratitude moment: How and why are you grateful for your innermost soul?

Closing reading: "Keep yourself clean and bright: you are the window through which you must see the world."
—George Bernard Shaw

Reflection: Journal, sketch, or in some way record your experience.

Intention: The next day, spend time engaged in something that feeds or inspires your soul.

Other focus aspects for additional holy nights:

- Balance
- Communication
- Compassion
- Contemplation
- Love
- Outreach
- Patience
- Personal growth
- Plenty
- Rebirth
- Scent
- Sight
- Silence and quiet
- Sound
- Struggle
- Taste
- Thought and cognition
- Vitality
- Warmth

A Winter Retreat

During winter's dark quiet, many Pagans feel an urge to reflect, make plans, and put their lives in order, and it's an urge underpinned by strong biological and magickal roots. For these reasons, winter is a powerful time for personal retreat.

What is retreat? Humans have long sought ways to separate themselves from their daily routines by turning inward. The monastic cloister, the vision quest, and even the vacation are all kinds of retreat. You can combine place, purpose, magickal practices, activities, and ritual to create your own winter retreat, focusing on settings and activities that correspond to the season. During your retreat, embrace and view the dark quiet of winter as a time for inward connection, planning, and tremendous personal growth. The body and mind are sanctuaries, and being able to feel spiritually whole—with an internal and external sense of peace and order—is vital to emotional health and security, particularly during winter, a time of year we instinctively associate with darkness and peril. You'll find your retreat will become a celebration.

Here are a few ideas for a winter retreat:

- Your retreat can occupy anything from a couple hours to a long weekend or even to several days. Choose a time and place in which you can be quiet, undisturbed, and need attend to no one but yourself. Let your loved ones know that you are to be undisturbed during this time.

- Honor the nature and value of silence and meditation as part of your retreat—both as a nod to winter's silence and also to benefit your own inward journey. Turn off electronic devices and resist the urge to use them through the retreat.

- Prepare for the retreat by gathering everything you'll need and purifying yourself in some way: shower, smudge, or whatever works for you.

- Open with a ritual or a simple statement of your purpose.

- Engage in activities that focus on planning, reflection, and person growth. Journaling and divination are fabulous winter retreat activities, as is planning a course of research or study. Some folks use winter retreat time to sew garb or create magickal tools.

- Work with magickal correspondences that link you to winter; see this book's correspondences for ideas.

- If you wish, carry out meditation, spellwork, or ritual to support your aims.

- If weather allows, consider a long, reflective walk outdoors, watching and listening for sights, sounds, and messages. Walks at the liminal times of sunrise and sunset will be especially wonderful.

- Bring light into your retreat with light strings, candles, or the magick of a hearth fire. Sit quietly with the light, enjoying its presence.

- Enjoy nutritious, healing foods to nurture your body and inspire your soul.

- Celebrate your retreat with a closing ritual, and if possible, create a small charm or talisman to keep with you as a reminder of the event.

And now, settle back and embrace the season. Turn off your cell phone, computer, and television and sit quietly with the lights or by the fire, contemplating the quiet depths of winter. Take walks. Feed the birds. Read a new book. Meditate. Play board games with your friends or family. Be grateful for the lessons of winter and joyous as you anticipate the return of the light.

RITUALS
OF
CELEBRATION

compassion, wisdom, insight, search for meaning, sacrifice, etc

...ion and looking inward, evaluation, reflection, meditation, hiber...

...n and scrying, study, journaling, tool crafting, feasting, comm...

work, deep ritual, vigil personal retreat, Amaterasu, Baba

...a, Bruno, Cailleach, Carlin, Carravogue, Ceres, Demeter, D...

...alda Koliada, Lachesis, Maryana, Rind Skadi, Snegu...

Bacchus, Hodlr, Lugh, Saturn, Dilis Varsvlavi, Cort, E...

...n Knight, Green Man, Holly King, Karkantzaros, Kne...

...Lutzelfrau, Pelznichol, Perchta, Samichlaus, Stallo, Tom...

...onn, Egregores, green: evergreen, abundance, life, new beginnings,

wealth, gifts, prosperity, solar energy, red: holly berries and...

...force, fire, white: silence, calm peace, protecting, cardamom: di...

...ticism, psychic powers, cinnamon: access to astral and spiritu...

...tuition strength, cloves: attraction, authority, healing power, ...

...th, intuition, renewal, transformation, vitality, mistletoe: peace,

...st, protection, nutmeg, alertness, awareness, inspiration, intelli...

...t calm, divination, intuition, psychic powers, relaxation, rosem...

...banishing, divination, healing, mental clarity, physical and...

...strength, sage: calm concentration, confidence, health, mon...

$\mathcal{H}$ERE WE ARE, in the book's final chapter, and it's time to talk about ritual and celebration. Pagans work rituals and hold festivities all the time, and these tend to take on a special focus at whatever we consider the "high holiday" times of the year. The Winter Solstice has always been prime time for celebration and ritual, thanks to its themes of rebirth, new life, and the solar return. In this chapter, we'll delve into some of these ideas and then offer specific suggestions for solo, group, and family celebrations.

First, let's consider the word "ritual." A ritual is a religious or solemn ceremony consisting of a series of actions performed in a prescribed order. The word comes from the root "rite," which relates to religious tradition or usage. Rituals always carry a specific purpose and may be enacted by one or more people. They may be planned to the last detail or may be completely spontaneous, and they typically have a beginning, middle, and end. Most Pagan rituals involve a raising of energy—they may also work with deities; involve prayer, petitions, initiations, blessings, or other intentional actions; or include divination. Rituals may be secular, but they more often have a religious or spiritual purpose.

Celebrations are a little different. The word comes from the Latin *celebrare*, which means, roughly, "frequented or honored." Celebrations tend to recognize important occasions and are often one-time events, as in the celebration that follows when one takes a new step in religious training or accepts a diploma or credential. Celebrations may have formal components, but typically they're more casual than structured rituals. They're rarely religious in nature, although they often occur in conjunction with religious rituals. A festivity is more or less the same as a celebration, although the word comes from a root meaning "feast" and suggesting a close relationship between celebration and food.

Let's explore this idea of a ritual or celebration being casual versus formal. I know a number of people who don't consider a ritual "valid" unless it involves a multipage script, heavily garbed participants, lots of cool props, and full memorization of parts. Oh—and it needs to last for at least an hour. Now, I'm not doubting the beauty and awe factor of a carefully choreographed, perfectly scripted, and completely memorized ritual, although sometimes when I watch one of these, I feel more like I'm watching a dramatic performance than a meaningful interaction with the divine. I've been involved in those mega rituals, and they've been interesting. Some have touched my soul. Then again, some of the most meaningful rituals I've taken part in were spur-of-the-moment and barely cohesive, yet overflowed with meaning.

People disagree, too, over whether ritual parts must be memorized. There are a lot of pluses to memorization: it looks smooth when players have their parts committed to memory, and it avoids the awkward squinting-at-note-cards or flapping-pieces-of-paper-around phenomena, which are distracting during ritual and look unprofessional. Memorization is also a great mental exercise, and if a part is memorized, one doesn't have to worry about forgetting to bring a set of note cards along. On the other hand, I would never cancel a ritual because someone didn't have a part memorized, nor would I hesitate to involve someone in a ritual at the last minute, handing him or her a written version of what they needed to read aloud.

Bottom line: these decisions are up to you, but they all must be carefully considered as you prepare your rituals. Consider the purpose for the ritual or celebration, who is involved, the setting, and what you need to accomplish. Respond accordingly, and in every case, make choices that are meaningful to you and those you're working with. If working with a group, make sure everyone understands the basic etiquette of your ritual workings—whether it is acceptable to carry magickal tools during the ritual, how to enter or leave a circle, and so forth.

Music in Ritual

The Winter Solstice and music go together, whether in the music we humans make or the otherworldly song created by the night wind blowing through winter evergreens. In the United States, most of us have grown up singing Christmas carols, regardless of our religious background. In times past, a carol was a combination of song and dance or of song and procession, traditions that led seamlessly into those of mummering and Morris dancing. Young children once honored the Winter Solstice with song, going throughout their villages and caroling door-to-door. The villagers rewarded them with tokens, sweets, and small gifts, symbolizing the food and prosperity given at Yule by the earth or Earth Mother to all her earthly children.

Mara Freeman recalls an early version of caroling, the Hebridean tradition of "Singing to the Son of the Dawn." A band of white-clad Christmas lads travels from house-to-house in their village. In each house they either lift up the smallest child or infant, or they fashion a holy infant out of a sheet or blanket. The infant was then carried around the hearth fire three times by the lads, while they sang a carol (Freeman, 354).

Even though the song was sung then as a Christmas carol, it was probably once an homage to the returning sun. In fact, the words come from one of the traditional chants written down by the Scottish folklorist Alexander Carmichael in his

Carmina Gadelica. The *Carmina* records Scottish folklore and traditions after the Christianization of the country; yet those traditions undoubtedly sprung from older Pagan ways, and so continue to reflect the past ways of those early people.

The tradition of caroling endures today, with singers often receiving cookies and cocoa at neighbors' doors. Many of what we think of as Christmas carols can be "Paganized" by changing the words a little bit. Some—such as "Deck the Halls" and "The Holly and the Ivy"—work as-is for Pagan singers. Caroling is also fabulous as another way for in-the-closet Pagans to celebrate in plain sight.

You may wish to supplement your ritual or celebration with instrumental music, too. Drums are said to represent Earth's heartbeat and are the instrument of the earth element. Using drums and percussion instruments in your ritual not only adds a lovely and mystical sound but also connects you to the earth and the forces of winter. Thanks to their versatility, stringed instruments are easy to bring along and can add immensely to your production. And bells, of course, are synonymous with winter—especially if you can round up some sleigh bells. Bells work wonderfully while proceeding to a ritual site or during the energy-raising phase. They're also known to magickally dispel negative energies from a space. And, they're just plain fun to work with.

Also, note that many traditional Christmas carols work perfectly well for the Pagan Midwinter, too. Some of the others can be "Paganized" to become perfect for Yule. An Internet search using the search string "Pagan carols Yule" will turn up dozens of resources from fellow Pagans who have already done much of this work for you.

Ah, the Planning...

As with planning any ritual, start with the basics, and then be sure that all participants are aware of the plan and their roles in it:

- What is the ritual's purpose? What do you hope to accomplish?
- When will you hold the ritual? Choose a date and time, and consider whether any special timing is needed.
- Where will you hold the ritual? Is weather an issue? Are any special permissions or preparations needed?
- Who will participate? Will children be involved?
- How will participants get there? Is parking available?
- What roles or speaking parts will the ritual have, and who will fill them? (Write out the plans in detail.)
- Are costumes, special attire, or props needed?
- Will there be music? Musical instruments?

- What magickal tools or supplies are needed?
- What about cakes and ale? What will you feature, and who will provide them?

The Role of Journaling in Ritual

Journaling is incredibly valuable in magickal practices of all types, and particularly when doing spellwork or ritual. When planning a ritual, use your journal to record the plan and its details, including the invocations, prayers, elemental calls, readings, or other scripted parts. Draw diagrams of your ritual site, the altar setup, or any other layouts that would be useful to recall in the future. As soon as you can after your ritual is complete, use your journal to capture your impression, feelings, and results of prayer or divination—your personal responses. Use the journal, too, to evaluate how well the ritual went in practical terms. What worked? What didn't? Would you change or add anything, or was it perfect? Making notes like these is pure gold in helping you develop a treasure chest of ritual practices. Returning to the journal to read your own impressions will help you track your own magickal growth and development.

The following are a set of preplanned rituals and celebrations. These are ready to use, but as with the spells, invocations, and other goodies in this book, you can modify these to fit your own needs—or use these ideas to create your own ground-up festivities!

A Fireside Festivity Ritual for Any Number of People

If you're lucky enough to have a fireplace, make use of it—everyone knows there's no better way to warm up a living space than with a warm, crackling fire on the hearth. Invite your friends to a "fireplace evening" of communal activities. An outdoor fire pit may work, too, depending on your weather. Here are a few suggestions for fireside festivity:

- Cook dinner over the fire, and follow it with storytelling. Ask each guest to come prepared with a story to tell. Perhaps offer a small Yule gift for the story everyone votes as best.

- Have a holiday game night! Prepare one or two games for everyone to play, and ask guests to bring sweet or savory snacks to share.

- Choose one or two holiday crafts that the group can do together. Even better: choose a craft that can be used to create holiday gifts. Finish with hot chocolate and holiday cookies.

A Midwinter Fire Ritual for a Solitary Practitioner

Purpose:

To welcome the coming of the solstice and return of the sun, and to reflect on the nature of this change and its deeper meanings.

Timing:

This ritual takes place on the Winter Solstice eve and requires about thirty to sixty minutes. It could easily be extended into an overnight vigil if you wish it. Assemble everything you need while it's still light out, and begin the ritual after dark.

Setting:

Outdoors if possible. If weather makes outdoor work prohibitive, use an indoor fireplace or a large candle set on a mirrored surface.

The directions given here correspond with earth as north, air as east, and so on. If your correspondences vary, adjust accordingly.

Supplies:

A fire pit, small fire-burning barbecue, or a large pillar candle
Kindling and firewood if lighting a fire
Matches and fire-safety equipment (shovel, pail of water)
A bell or sleigh bells
Small scrolls of paper on which you have written statements
   or wishes to "give" to the fire (see preparations)
Your favorite method of divination
Offerings to deity (this is optional—only if it's something you
   wish to do)
A lantern or headlamp
A chair or camp-style chair (set next to the fire pit)
Cakes and ale (using holiday goodies)

Pre-Ritual Preparation:

Washing with frankincense soap is the perfect way to purify and prepare oneself before the ritual. Wear whatever garb and jewelry suit you, but be wary of not having sweeping robes or cloaks near open fire.

Preparations:

Before the ritual, take small pieces of paper and on them, write anything you would like to "let go" of during the ritual. The light is returning: what bits of "darkness" do you wish to offer to the fire and the returning sun?

If using a fire, lay it carefully before your ritual begins, designing it so it is easy to light with one match.

The Ritual:

After dark, proceed to the ritual site, using as little light as possible. (But be safe: better to wear a headlamp if you need one than to fall down and break something. Common sense rules! You could also mark the path with a few widely-spaced luminarias; the low light next to the ground will maintain darkness, and they're beautiful, too.) Be silent as you walk.

When you reach the site, repeat the following, from Victor Hugo: *"It seemed to be a necessary ritual that he should prepare himself for sleep by meditating under the solemnity of the night sky... a mysterious transaction between the infinity of the soul and the infinity of the universe."* (Note: adjust the pronouns as needed.)

Begin by facing east. It's customary, but not required, to raise your hands to the element or direction as you speak. In your own words—which you may write out in advance or simply speak spontaneously in the moment—speak to and welcome the air element. You might comment on the evanescence of air, lightness of being, awakening, and transformation. Pause for a moment; listen, feel, and open yourself to the east, and consider what gifts it brings into your life. Here is a sample directional elemental call for the east:

> *Element of the east,*
> *place of air, the breath of life,*
> *that which we cannot see*
> *but which fills us with life*
> *and infuses us with inspiration,*
> *be with us now.*

Turn to your right to face the south. Repeat the same welcome, this time mentioning the fire passions, the weight and life itself, the warmth of the hearth fire, and the return of the life-giving sun. Here is a sample directional elemental call for the south:

> *Element of the south,*
> *place of fire, heat of heart's blood,*
> *that which courses through us,*
> *filling us with passion*
> *and infusing us with life-giving heat,*
> *be with us now.*

Turn to the right again, facing west. Repeat the same welcome, this time mentioning the restless, transformative shape-shifting of water into winter ice and snow, and the way it wanders, always seeking new paths. Here is a sample directional elemental call for the west:

Element of the west,
place of water, shape-shifting,
that which constantly moves and transforms,
nurturing creativity
and gifting us with fresh vision,
be with us now.

Finally turn to the north, the direction given to the earth element and to winter. Speak of challenges, endings and beginnings, death and birth, and eternity. Mention the gifts of earth, and the hope they will be given again in the common year. Here is a sample directional elemental call for the east:

Element of the north,
place of grounding, place of birth,
fierce winter land of ice and cold,
endings and beginnings,
always calling us home,
be with us now.

Pause now, settle into your chair, and fold your arms around your chest. Make yourself as small as possible. Focus on feeling the darkness and cold. If you wish to, pray or meditate at this point. You may also use this time to invite your chosen deities to join you in the ritual space. (And remember: always invite—never demand.)

When ready, stand up, turn to your fire pit, and light the fire (or its substitute). As the fire begins to burn, circle it sunwise (deosil), repeating this chant:

Yuletide wisdom,
Yuletide cheer,
winter's spirit,
welcome here!

You may also choose to sing a winter carol or use a difference chant if you wish. Continue circling and singing, ringing your bell as you do. When the fire (or you!) seems to reach its peak, stop, and focus for a moment on feeling its warmth, and how different the heated energy feels compared to the cold sojourn in your chair. Feel your warmth and imagine your life's blood coursing through your veins. Lift your arms first to the fire and then to the sky. While you were in your chair, folded up into a ball, you were like the cold, sleeping earth. Now you are the returning sun, boundless in heat and energy!

Taking your scrolls, toss them into the fire one by one, saying with each: *I release these to the return of the light!* As you do, think hard about what you're letting go, visualizing the separation and thinking about what this means to you.

If you have invited deities to the fire, now would be a good time to commune with them and do whatever work needs to be done.

Before the fire begins to die down, pick up your divination tool of choice and do a quick reading. Some people use the results as an assessment of how effective the ritual has been. If the reading is "lacking," they do a bit more energy raising or perhaps add a new appeal to deity, then they repeat the reading to see if it is now more favorable. Others use the chance to take a reading on the coming post-solstice season, testing the waters to see what lies ahead.

As the fire begins to subside, take a seat in your chair and enjoy your cakes and ale with a sense of peaceful gratitude. Sit by the fire until it has faded to coals. (If using candles, sit for as long as you wish.)

Complete your ritual with a statement of thanks or gratitude. "Release" the elements, working counterclockwise (widdershins) from north to west to south to east, thanking the forces at each point. Here is a sample directional elemental call for release:

Element of the [name the direction],
I am grateful for your presence here.
Please go in peace, as will I.

Ideally, don't throw water on your fire—it should burn out naturally. Do not leave it unattended! A happy medium is to use a shovel to gently spread the coals and rake dirt or ashes over them, working deosil around the fire ring until no coals are visible, and only then sprinkling the pit with water. If using candles, pinch them out with a wet finger or use a candlesnuffer—never blow them out.

Variation: If you have an intrepid spirit and can manage to stay awake all night, you might try keeping a fire vigil. Sitting vigil means sitting by the fire through the night and awaiting the rising Winter Solstice sun. If you plan to do this, you'll need more food and lots more firewood—and be sure to add plenty of blankets or a sleeping bag. As you sit vigil, you might journal, read, work with divination, or simply sit with your thoughts. Greet the winter sunrise with singing and cheering, then treat yourself to a full-on breakfast. (And a nap!)

Variation: Use the contemplative portion of your ritual to write goals or resolutions for the coming year.

Variation: This could easily be made into a group ritual, having different people do the elemental calls, lead the energy raising, invite deities, etc.

A Midwinter Yule Log Ritual for Two People

A Yule log ritual is a terrific way for two people to celebrate, whether spouses, friends, or partners. It's formal yet informal, it's very much a part of the season, and it's just plain cozy.

Purpose:

To honor Midwinter and the tradition of the Yule log, which is said to bring luck, grant protection, and furnish insights.

Timing:

The Yule log is traditionally burned on solstice eve, but this ritual could easily be done at any time during the Midwinter season. It will be most effective at night.

Supplies:

Evergreen soap (or smudge)

A Yule log—Your Yule log can be an actual log (oak, if possible) or it could be a piece of wood designated for the purpose. Be sure it is dry, aged wood, and consider how long you want it to burn. If you have no way to provide an actual log, consider one of those three-hour fireplace logs. A small log will last through a short evening ritual. If you want the log to burn all night, it will need to be *big*, and you'll need a lot of smaller firewood to help it ignite.

A fireplace (if you want to be inside) or a fire pit or small fire-burning barbecue (for an outdoor ritual)

Matches and fire-safety equipment

Pocketknife

Permanent markers

Pieces of colored paper

String

Red ribbons

Scissors

Evergreen sprigs or trimmings

Essential oils

Libation (ale, mead, or whiskey)

Two acorns (or paper representations)

Two glasses

Cakes and ale (using holiday goodies)

Pre-Ritual Preparation:

Wash with an evergreen-scented soap or use an evergreen smudge to purify before the ritual. Dress casually and wear magickal jewelry—you will be working with wood and knives (not the best time for formal garb or flowing sleeves).

Trim the log to fit your fireplace, and assemble all of the other materials near your fireplace. Memorize any of the readings or write them in bold marker on index cards (so they'll be easy to see in the dark).

Think in advance of what things you would like to let go of and what wishes and goals you have for the coming year. Make a list that you can read from during the ritual.

The Ritual:

The ritual begins when the two of you carry the log together —each holding an end—and set it before the fireplace. As you do, say:

> *The Wheel turns and turns and then,*
> *we turn the Wheel once again.*

Working together, adorn the log. Follow the ideas from the *Recipes and Crafts* chapter to carve an image of the Cailleach, add other inscriptions, or tie on wishes and ribbons. You might anoint the log with evergreen oils and tie on sprigs of greenery, asking for the protection of the evergreen trees. Work together, talking as you do, sharing ideas and recalling stories from past winters. This is all part of the ritual. Finish with a drizzle of ale or whiskey—an offering to the spirit within the log.

When you're finished, put the log in place and lay a smaller fire around it. The small fire's purpose is to ignite the larger log.

Both of you, together, should speak aloud the traditional story of the Yule log. Then, extinguish all the lights in the room and sit quietly together in the darkness, each contemplating the past calendar year—the challenges as well as the good times—and each imagining what you would wish for in the coming year.

When you're ready, light the fire together. (If you want to be really cool, use flint and steel or another match-free technique.) As it begins to burn, throw in more dried evergreen sprigs and say farewell to the old year. Your farewells can be a combination of thanks and appreciations as well as banishment of old habits or personal pains. Take turns offering your farewells, feeding the small fire with wood as it grows in strength.

Once the Yule log itself begins blazing, it's time to contemplate the year ahead and the power of possibilities. Watch as your carvings and offerings are burned, imaging your wishes being carried skyward. Speak aloud:

As you burn, our thoughts go free.
As we will, so mote it be!

Throw your acorns into the fire to represent the year ahead, and speak aloud your plans, wishes, resolutions, and hopes. Enjoy a period of silent fire scrying, seeing what mysteries you can find within the flames.

Pour yourselves two glasses of libation and toast the coming year and each other. If you feel like it, sing a song over the burning log. The traditional carol, "Deck the Halls," is good because it mentions the solstice, the change in the solar year, and the Yule log. Enjoy your cakes and ale.

If possible, let the Yule log burn down to a few chunks of charred wood and ashes—depending on your time frame, you may end the ritual long before the log burns down. If you plan to sit up with the log through the night, raise the lights a bit and enjoy telling stories or playing parlor games. Following an ancient tradition, save remnants of the fire and use them to start the Yule log fire the following year.

Variation: You may wish to exchange gifts as part of the ceremony. You might gives gifts that specifically represent the coming year in some way.

A Yule Ritual: The Return of the Light for a Family or Group

This ritual is aimed at honoring the sun's return. It is simple, yet meaningful, and it can be done inside or outside—a benefit in inclement weather.

Purpose:

To welcome the returning light and focus on the spirit of the season.

Setting:

This can be done at any time during the Midwinter season. It would be especially effective on the solstice eve. This is designed to be done indoors.

Supplies:

A large table (or two or three card tables)

One white candle for each group or family member

A larger or taller yellow or gold "solar candle"

A candle holder for each candle

A large mirror (or mirrors), on which the candles will be set

Matches

Two large baskets or decorative boxes

Candlesnuffer

Several large darning needles

Black permanent markers

Paper towels

Various themed holiday decorations, such as white or gold glass balls, winter figures, or pieces of white, gold, or red ribbon

A source of light (if outside)

Cakes and ale (from holiday goodies)

Pre-Ritual Preparation:

Participants should purify using their favorite methods. Attire can be *ad lib* or everyone could be asked to wear a certain type of garb, a specific color, etc. All should be aware of not allowing draping sleeves to catch fire while working around multiple candles.

Prepare an altar by placing the table in the center of the ritual space, leaving enough space for participants to easily circle and move around the table. Place the mirror in the center of the table. Set the gold candle on the mirror; set the matches and snuffer to one side. Place the needles, sharpies, and white candles in one basket or decorative box and place the holiday decorations in the second basket/box; set both off to one side.

Divide the individual speaking parts or actions. Each person should prepare by studying the history of Yule and bringing some pieces of Yule knowledge or traditions to share during the ritual. Each person should bring two or more holiday decorations for the table. These could be glass balls (especially in gold), winter figurines, appropriate deity statuary, or anything else related to the solstice and the sun. (Avoid paper decorations near the candle flames.)

Each person should bring a small inexpensive wrapped gift. If there is to be any special "theme" to these gifts, participants should know in advance. These gifts should be age and gender-appropriate to all participants.

Participants will have a chance during the ritual to offer personal prayers, petitions, etc.—be sure they know this in advance. Participants may be invited to bring a holiday treat to share for cakes and ale. Be aware of any specific dietary requirements within the group.

The Ritual:

Have everyone gather away from the ritual site and proceed to the site while singing a holiday carol. Pick one that already works for the Pagan Yule, like "Drum the Sun" from the website Pagan Hymns, Carols, and other Assorted Songs. Participants should carry their wrapped gifts. As they reach the site, they should circle around the table, placing their gifts underneath it.

One participant should offer an invocation to the sun. After this is complete, everyone should say together: *"Welcome, sun!"*

One participant says: *Let us come together and prepare glorious lights to entice the sun's return.*

At this time, participants begin decorating the candles. Each person should use the darning needles to etch symbols, sigils, or words into their candle. (For extra fun, work with magickal alphabets—you can provide sheets for people to use.) They could also simply etch images of the sun and its rays. Encourage people to make these ornate, with lots of designs, borders, etc. Participants can watch each other work and get ideas on the spot. This should take a fair amount of time and should not be rushed—this creative aspect of the ritual is very important, for everyone's energies are being invested in the sun's return.

When finished etching, each participant should use a permanent marker to color over the carvings, which will fill with the marker's ink. A paper towel should then be used to rub off the excess. The etched candles will now sport decorative, ink-filled etchings. Have participants place their candles in holders (if needed) and set them around the edges of the mirror.

Next, everyone will work together to decorate/etch the solar candle. Working one at a time, each person should step to the table, make some sort of mark or design on the candle, and etch his or her name. As each person finishes, she holds the candle aloft and explains to the group the designs she added. She then offers the candle to the next person, who steps forward and repeats the process.

When the final person has finished decorating the solar candle, he or she places it in a holder and sets it on the mirror in the center of the other candles.

One participant says: *Let us come together and prepare beautiful decorations to entice the sun's return.*

All step up to the table and work together, adding decorations from the second basket—balls, figurines, ribbons, or whatever else is at hand—to turn the table in a brilliantly festive space. The candle layout now represents the dazzling potential of the rising sun.

One person says the following: *We come together tonight to honor the tradition of Midwinter as a solar holiday and to welcome the sun's return.*

At this point, turn off the lights and stand in darkness for a few moments.

While the others stand in darkness, one person says the following: *We feel the darkness of this time of year. The days are short, the sun is low, and the nights are long. The trees fall bare, and animals sleep beneath the snow. We feel the cold and miss the sun's life-giving warmth. We recognize winter's peril. The world goes quiet, and each day, each night, we contemplate the sun's importance to all life. We dream of warmth, yearning for the end of the long nights and the rebirth of the life-giving sun!*

The youngest person present should then light the solar candle (with help, if this participant is a child).

As the solar candle is lit, one participant says: *Behold the light. Let us be silent in its presence while we contemplate this gift.*

All wait silently.

One participant reads aloud a version of "Raven, Bringer of the Light" (see *New Ways* chapter for one version of this traditional tale).

Moving around the circle deosil (sunwise), each individual steps up to the table, lights his or her candle from the solar candle, and sets the candle back in position. As each candle is lit, everyone says: *The light returns anew.*

When all of the candles are lit, the participants join hands and walk deosil around the table, singing a joyous holiday carol to raise energy. This can continue for as long as desired; one person should be responsible for bringing it to a close.

Anyone who desires may, at this time, offer spontaneous prayers, petitions, or blessings.

One participant says: *Let the returning sun now share in our merriment!*

And now the fun begins! (People may wish to sit on the floor or in chairs during this part of the ritual.) Working deosil, and starting with the oldest person present, each participant in turn should share a bit of knowledge about Yule or the solstice, tell a story, describe a traditional practice, etc. As each person finishes, he or she takes one of the gifts from under the table. Once all the gifts have been taken, the person sharing a bit of knowledge may swap gifts with anyone else in the circle—which will be done with great hilarity! Keep this going until no one has anything more to offer or until enough time has gone by (designate one person to be the determiner of when the gift swap should end, or predetermine a number of "rounds" for the trivia contest).

Everyone now opens their gifts and enjoys the merrymaking. Share cakes and ale, leaving the candles burning to show the joy in the sun's return.

To finish, everyone joins hands and sings a song. The carol, "We Wish You a Merry Christmas" can be adapted to "We Wish You a Merry Solstice" and sung to end the ritual.

Each participant, moving deosil, shall step up to the table and extinguish their candle with the snuffer.

One participant shall be given the honor of extinguishing the solar candle. As this is done, everyone should repeat: *Go in peace.*

The ritual is now complete. Participants may continue to visit and enjoy the evening and their gifts, and each one takes his or her own white candle home at evening's end.

Variation: Instead of bringing actual gifts, participants could choose a word or phrase (e.g., "love," "prosperity," "kindness of strangers," "light in the darkness"), inscribe it on a small scroll, and wrap it in a small gift box.

Variation: With some modification, this ritual could be done outside—and it would be gorgeous on a clear, starlit night!

And here we are, at the end of things. May you have a good Yule and a blessed return of the sun!

CORRESPONDENCES
FOR
YULE

...ression, wisdom, insight, search for meaning, sacrifice, eternity

...and looking inward, evaluation, reflection, meditation, hibernati...

...d scrying, study, journaling, tool crafting, feasting, communal

...k, deep ritual, vigil personal retreat, Amaterasu, Baba Yag...

...Brum, Cailleach, Carlin, Carravogue, Ceres, Demeter, Decim...

...Koliada, Lachesis, Marzana, Rind Skadi, Snegurochk...

...chus, Hodler, Lugh, Saturn, Delis Varsolar, Cert, Ebus...

...Knight, Green Man, Holly King, Karkantzaros, Knecht

...tzelfrau, Pelznichol, Perchta, Samichlaus, Stallo, Tomten,

...Egregores, green: evergreen, abundance, life, new beginnings, wea...

...lth, gifts, prosperity, solar energy, red: holly berries and poin...

...fire, white: silence, calm peace, protecting, cardamom: divina...

...n, psychic powers, cinnamon: access to astral and spiritual re...

...en strength, cloves: attraction, authority, healing power, protec...

...ntuition, renewal, transformation, vitality, mistletoe: peace, pro...

...protection, nutmeg, alertness, awareness, inspiration, intelligence,

...calm, divination, intuition, psychic powers, relaxation, rosemary:...

...thing, divination, healing, mental clarity, physical and psychi...

...wealth, 1969, calm concentration, purifying, health...

Spiritual Focus and Key Words

Beginnings

birth

challenge

compassion

cycles

endings

eternity

gratitude

insight

rebirth

restoration

sacrifice

search for meaning

silence

sleep

wisdom

Magickal Focus and Suggested Workings

Communal celebration

contemplation and looking inward

deep ritual

divination and scrying

evaluation

feasting ("Eat, drink, and be merry!")

healing work

hibernation (falling into "sync" with darkness)

journaling

meditation

reflection

study

"taking stock"

tool crafting

vigil, personal retreat

Astrological timing

The origins of the word *Yule* are not clearly known, but the word is most often interpreted as meaning "wheel," whether in terms of the turning of the seasons, the circular motion of the sun, or the wheels of Odin's chariot. Yule was originally a Wiccan term; it's now widely used by the general Pagan community to describe the winter holiday occurring at or around the time of the astronomical Winter Solstice.

Astronomically, the Winter Solstice represents the longest night and shortest day in the Northern Hemisphere and occurs on Dececmber 21–22. The Winter Solstice occurs in the Northern Hemisphere when the sun reaches its negative-most (or southernmost) point over the North Pole, relative to the Summer Solstice. To viewers on Earth, the Winter Solstice sun rises to its lowest point in the midday sky, and because its arc is so low, it appears to pause. The word "solstice" comes from Latin roots meaning "sun stopped" or "sun stands still."

Astrologically, the Winter Solstice corresponds with the movement of the sun into the astrological sign of Capricorn.

Archetypes
FEMALE
The holy mother (from the German *heilig*, "whole"), who births light back into the world, often in the form of a child

MALE
Father Time
the Green Knight as the spirit of winter incarnate
the King, a mature male and oft-solar deity

Deities and Heroes
GODDESSES
Amaterasu (Japan)
Baba Yaga (Slavic)

Befana (Italian)

Bona Dea (ancient Roman)

Brimo (Greek)

Cailleach (Celtic)

Carlin (Scot version of the Cailleach)

Carravogue (Ireland and Britain)

Ceres (Roman)/Demeter (Greek)

Decima (Roman)

Fauna (Roman)

Holda (aka Frau Holle; Germany)

Koliada (aka Koleda; pre-Christian Slavic)

Lachesis (Greek)

Marzana, aka Moranna (Baltic/Slavic)

Rind (Scandinavia)

Skadi (Scandinavia)

Snegurochka (Russia)

Tonan (Aztec)

Gods

Bacchus (Roman; often linked to winter via feasting and
    drinking)

Hodhr (aka Hod, Hoder, Hodur; Norse)

Saturn or Saturnus (Roman; Lord of Capricorn)

MAGICKAL BEINGS

Cert (aka Krampus)

Dilis Varsvlavi (Georgian mythos)

Elves

Gawain the Green Knight (Arthurian legend)

the Green Man

the Holly King, who is said to surrender to the Oak King at
the Winter Solstice

Karkantzaros (Greek)

Knecht Ruprecht (German)

Lucka (Bohemia)

the Lutzelfrau (German)

the Pelznichol, Perchta (aka Bertha; German)

Samichlaus (Swiss)

the Stallo (Sami)

Tomten (including the Nisse and the Tonttu; Scandinavian)

Weihnachtsmann (German; the "gift man")

Egregores: Santa Claus!

Archaeoastronomical Sites

Almendres Cromlech (Portugal)

Cahokia Mounds (Missouri, US)

Chaco Canyon (New Mexico, US)

Chichen Itza (Mexico, Yucatán peninsula)

Easter Island (Polynesia)

Glastonbury (Britain)

Goseck Circle (Germany)

Kastelli jätinkirkko (Finland)

Machu Picchu (Peru)

Newgrange (Ireland; part of the Brú na Bóinne complex)

Stonehenge (Britain)

Tikal (Guatemala)

Colors

Green: Abundance, life, the living evergreen that thrives through the winter, new beginnings, wealth

Gold: Gifts, prosperity, richness, solar energy wealth; associated with gods, kings, and royalty

Red: vitality, fire (inner and outer), life force; associated with holly berries and poinsettias, plants that thrive during winter

White: Calm, the "clean slate" of snow peace, protecting, silence

Herbs and Spices

Cardamom: Divination, intuition, mysticism, psychic powers

Cinnamon: Access to astral and spiritual realms, authority, intuition, psychic powers, strength

Cloves: Attraction, authority, divination, healing, power, protection, psychic powers, purification

Ivy: Birth, intuition, rebirth, renewal, transformation, vitality

Mistletoe: healing, peace, prosperity, protection, rest, wellness; also believed to be an aphrodisiac

Nutmeg: Alertness, awareness, inspiration, intelligence, intuition

Peppermint: Calm, divination, intuition, psychic powers, relaxation

Rosemary: Alertness, banishing, divination, healing, mental clarity, physical and psychic protection, strength

Sage (culinary): Calm, concentration, confidence, divination, health and healing, protection, satisfaction

Saffron: Intense emotion, passion, prosperity, sensitivity, wealth

Trees

Evergreens: natural symbols of rebirth and resurrection, and life everlasting

Cedar: Banishing, courage, determination, discipline, healing, longevity, prosperity, purification

Fir: Calm, comfort, guardianship, kingship, intuition, protection

Pine: Fertility, health and healing, prosperity, protection

Spruce: Adaptability, clarity, grounding, perseverance, protection, strength

Holly: Luck, protection, reconciliation, strength, web-weaving, wisdom, wishes

Pecan: Abundance, longevity, prosperity, success

Flowers

Christmas rose: Protection, strength, tenacity

Poinsettia: Chakra balancing, energy enhancement

Crystals and Stones

Onyx: Balance between physical and spiritual energy, grounding, protecting

Tanzanite: Dispels negativity, lifts depression, mental clarity

Turquoise: Contentment, healing, power, protection

Zircon: Calming, healing

Metals

Gold: Authority, creativity, fortune, hope, solar and masculine energies success, wealth

Lead: Banishing, centering, earth correspondences, focus, grounding, perseverance, protection, stability

Animals, Totems, and Mythical Creatures

Bear: The hibernating bear is revered as the symbol of winter incarnate, for when bears emerge from their period of winter hibernation, light and life have clearly returned to the earth.

Cows and oxen: Important symbols of food and wealth. The period around the Winter Solstice is the traditional time of the "culling of the herds," when animals were selected for butchering.

Flying reindeer: the powerful stag given wings!

Horse: Sacred to many cultures and involved in a ritual known as "Hoodening," in which a man costumed as a horse goes door-to-door, collecting money in exchange for entertainment.

Pigs: Often seen on feast tables, pigs are very intelligent and are long revered as powerful, sacred animals. The ancient Celts believed pigs to be a sacred gift from the otherworld. The Norse god of sunshine, Frey, road across the sky on the back of a gold-bristled boar, *Gulli-burstin*, whose spikey bristles looked like the sun's rays.

Raven: Credited by many aboriginal traditions as both trickster and bringer of light and thus is deeply associated with the Winter Solstice.

Reindeer and stag: Symbols of the Forest God and the Horned God, i.e., he who reigns during winter. A white doe is synonymous with a mother figure or mother goddess.

Changes and adaptations animals demonstrate in winter: Camouflage, hibernation, migration, thickening of coat, torpor. These changes demonstrate resilience and self-preservation.

Guising: The act of disguising oneself as an animal. This allowed aboriginal humans to honor totem creatures and to enact the idea of sacrifice by becoming symbolically related to the animals that sustained them through the winter. Processions of animal guisers found their way into the winter rituals of many cultures. Guising still goes on today, usually in conjunction with mummer plays and Morris dancing.

Scents for Oils, Incense, Potpourri, or Just Floating in the Air

Cardamom

cinnamon

clove

evergreens (fir, pine, spruce, and cedar)

frankincense

myrrh

wood smoke

Tarot Keys

The Hermit

the Magician

Pentacles

the World

Symbols and Tools

Cauldron: Deep insights, psychic stirring, intuition, self-knowledge, creation, manifestation

Darkness: Quiet, solitude, exploration, revealing of the unknown

Evergreens/greenery: Tenacity, strength, rebirth, cycle of life, fertility, fidelity, purification (especially cedar)

Light: Rebirth, renewal, energy, solar return, inspiration, initiation

Mother and child: Birth and life cycles describing the turning of the seasonal wheel, regeneration, fertility, family

Trees: Tenacity, strength, wisdom, endurance, knowledge, regeneration

Wreaths: The everlasting circle, magickal or sacred space, community, celebration

Yule log: Cleansing, blessing, the embodiment of winter/cold/death, augury, luck

Foods

Bûche de Noël (roasts of meat and poultry)

citrus fruits

fruitcake

homemade baked goods

scalloped, mashed, roasted, or *au gratin* root vegetables (potatoes, rutabagas, turnips, parsnips, sweet potatoes)

Drinks

Drinking vinegars

eggnog

glug

hot buttered rum

hot coffee drinks

hot chocolate

hot toddy (lemon, honey, alcohol, boiling water, and a cinnamon stick)

mulled wine

tea

Tom and Jerry

wassail

Activities and Traditions of Practice

Decorating the homestead, making and giving gifts, baking soul cakes, attending live performances and concerts (traditional: Mummer plays and Morris dancing), watching the Gemini meteor showers (December 12–14), game playing, caroling, bonfires and fire circles, storytelling, ringing of bells, "first footing" (on New Year's), and all varieties of ritual (solo and communal) and "high celebration."

Acts of Service

Giving to those less fortunate

feeding birds and wildlife (while following sustainable
practices)

furnishing warm clothing for those in need

sending packages to military personnel overseas

working in food banks and soup kitchens

Alternate Names for Yule in Other Traditions and Cultures

Alban Aretha ("druidic" per the writings of Iola Morganwyg;
although most of Morganwyg's works have been found to
be self-created, many still follow his teachings)

December solstice (used to clarify Northern/Southern Hemisphere meanings)

Dongzhi Festival: (December 22; China and other Asian
countries)

Goru (December 21; Mali)

Inti Raymi (June 21–24, Peru)

Midvinterblot (December 21; Norse)

Midwinter

Natalis Sol Invictus—Birth of the Unconquered Sun (December 21 Etruscan. Roman)

Soyal (December 21; Zuni and Hopi)

We Tripantu (June 21–24; Chile)

Winter Solstice (December 21–22; marks the time of the longest night and shortest day in the Northern Hemisphere)

Winternights

Yalda (December 21; Iran)

Yulefest, Yuletide

Ziemassvētki (December 22; ancient Latvia)

Holidays or Traditions Occurring During Yule in the Northern Hemisphere:

RELIGIOUS

Brumalia (Often began at the end of November and extended into January)

Saṅghamittā (First full moon in December; Sri Lanka)

Chalica (First week in December; Unitarian Universalists)

St. Barbara's Day (December 4; Christian; once a church-sponsored holiday, the day is now celebrated by a number of traditions)

Advent (Christian; date varies, but involves the four Sundays before Christmas)

Chanukah/Hanukkah (variable date; Jewish)

St. Nicholas' Day (December 6)

Bodhi Day (December 8; Buddha's enlightenment)

Our Lady of Guadalupe (December 12; Mexican)

St. Lucia's Day (December 13; Swedish)

Las Posadas (December 16–24; Mexico)

Saturnalia (December 17–23; Roman)

Koruchan (December 21; Eastern European- Slavic)

Pancha Ganapati (December 21–25; US Hindus)

Koliada (aka Koleda; once ancient but now celebrated around
December 24 in modern Slavic countries)

Christmas (December 25)

Mother's Night or Modranicht (December 27; Saxon)

Twelvetide (Twelve Days of Christmas)

Twelfth Night (night of January 5)

Epiphany (January 6)

SECULAR

Deuorius Riuri (Ancient Gaul)

Krampusnacht (December 6; Alpine Europe)

Feast of Fools (Variable times beginning in mid-December;
wild communal parties, sprouting up around the time of
the Winter Solstice; medieval Europe)

Burning of the Clocks (December 21–22; Brighton, United
Kingdom)

Festivus (December 23; United States)

Kwanzaa (December 26; Pan-African holiday celebrated in
North America)

Boxing Day (December 26; United Kingdom, Australia,
Canada, and New Zealand)

Junkanoo (December 26; Caribbean countries)

Wren Day or *Lá an Dreoilín* (December 26; Ireland, the Isle of Man and Wales)

Watch Night (December 31)

Hogmanay and "First Footing" (Night of December 31 to dawn on January 1; Scotland)

New Year's Eve and Day (December 31 and January 1)

Distaff Day (January 7; also called Roc Day; European nations)

Holidays or Traditions Occurring During Yule in the Southern Hemisphere:

RELIGIOUS

Vestalia, the Festival of Vesta (June 7–15)

St. Alban's Day (June 20 or 22)

Gwyl o Cerridwen (Feast of Cerridwen; modern Welsh witchcraft, July 13)

SECULAR

Fête de la Musique (World Music Day June 21)

Indians Day or Peasants Day (June 24; Peru)

Canada Day (July 1)

US Independence Day (July 4)

French Bastille Day (July 14)

FURTHER READING

Books

Campbell, Joseph. The Hero with a Thousand Faces. Princeton, NJ: Princeton University Press, 1972.

Edwards, Carolyn McVickar. The Return of the Light: Twelve Tales from Around the World for the Winter Solstice. New York: Marlowe and Company, 2000.

Grossman, John. Christmas Curiosities: Odd, Dark, and Forgotten Christmas. New York: Stewart, Tabori, and Chang, 2008.

Jackson, Sophie. The Medieval Christmas. Gloucestershire, UK: Sutton, 2005.

Llewellyn's Sabbat Series. Published Annually; Varied Authors. Woodbury, MN: Llewellyn.

Raedisch, Linda. The Old Magic of Christmas: Yuletide Traditions for the Darkest Days of the Year. Woodbury, MN: Llewellyn, 2013.

Rätsch, Christian, and Claudia Müller-Ebeling. Pagan Christmas: The Plants, Spirits, and Rituals at the Origins of Yuletide. Rochester, VT: Inner Traditions, 2006.

Online

Chambers, Robert. The Book of Days. Accessed April 27, 2015. http://www.thebookofdays.com.

Fitzgerald, Waverly. "Winter Solstice Blessings." School of the Seasons. December 20, 2008. http://www.schoolofthe-seasons.com/newletters/news122008.html.

Miles, Clement A. Christmas in Ritual and Tradition, Christian and Pagan. Project Gutenberg [EBook #19098]. August 21, 2006. http://www.gutenberg.org.

BIBLIOGRAPHY

Books

Armour, Robert A. *Gods and Myths of Ancient Egypt*. Cairo: American University in Cairo Press, 2001.

Bridge, James. "St. Lucy." *The Catholic Encyclopedia (Vol. 9)*. (New York: Appleton, 1910/2013).

Clauss, Manfred. *The Roman Cult of Mithras: The God and His Mysteries*. Translated by Richard Gordon. Edinburgh: Edinburgh University Press, 2000.

Danaher, Kevin. *The Year in Ireland: Irish Calendar Customs*. Minneapolis, MN: Mercier Press, 1972.

Frazer, Sir James G. *The Golden Bough*. Los Angeles: Gramercy, 1993.

Freeman, Mara. *Kindling the Celtic Spirit: Ancient Traditions to Illumine Your Life Through the Seasons*. San Francisco: HarperSanFrancisco, 2000.

Henes, Donna. *Celestially Auspicious Occasions: Seasons, Cycles & Celebrations*. New York: Perigee, 1996.

Hopman, Ellen Evert. *A Druid's Herbal for the Sacred Earth Year*. Rochester, VT: Destiny Books, 1994.

———. *Scottish Herbs and Fairy Lore*. Los Angeles: Pendraig, 2010.

Jung, Carl. *The Portable Jung*. New York: Penguin, 1976.

Lindow, John. *Norse Mythology: A Guide to the Gods, Heroes, Rituals, and Beliefs*. New York: Oxford University Press USA, 2001).

Matthews, John. *The Winter Solstice: The Sacred Traditions of Christmas*. Wheaton, IL: Quest Books, 1998.

McNeill, F. Marian. *The Silver Bough, Vol. 1: Scottish Folklore and Folk-Belief*. Reprint ed. Edinburgh: Canongate, 2001.

Pesznecker, Susan. *The Magickal Retreat: Making Time for Solitude, Intention, & Rejuvenation*. Woodbury, MN: Llewellyn, 2012.

Smith, William. *Dictionary of Greek and Roman Biography and Mythology*. Reprint ed. London: Tauris, 2007.

Wallis, Faith, trans. *Bede: The Reckoning of Time.* Liverpool: Liverpool University Press, 1999/2004.

Online

Bennett, Chris. "Roman Dates. Eponymous Years." Last modified January 25, 2012. http://www.tyndalehouse.com/Egypt/ptolemies/chron/roman/chron_rom_cal.htm#eponymous.

Collier, Kevin. "Countless Students Participate in 'Snow Day' Ritual." Last revised December 17, 2012. http://www.grandhaventribune.com/article/strange-grand-haven/265096.

Cooper, James. "The History of Wassailing and Mumming." Accessed April 27, 2015. http://www.whychristmas.com/customs/wassailing.shtml.

Dashu, Max. "The Women's Mysteries: Bona Dea." Last modified 2004. http://www.suppressedhistories.net/secrethistory/womensmysteries.html.

The European Graduate School. "Democritus Quotes." Accessed April 27, 2015. http://www.egs.edu/library/democritus/quotes/.

Freeman, Mara. "December: Winter Solstice." Chalice Centre. Last revised 2013. http://www.chalicecentre.net/december-celtic-year.html.

Greek and Roman Mythology; The Department of Classical Studies Dictionary. "Strenae." Last modified 2015, http://www.classics.upenn.edu/myth/php/tools/dictionary.php?regexp=FASTI.&method=standard.

Greek Mythology. "The Fates." Last modified 2014, http://www.greekmythology.com/Other_Gods/The_Fates/the_fates.html.

Hugo, Victor. "'Stellar' Quotes Throughout History." The Horizons Observatory. Accessed April 28, 2015. http://www.horizonsobservatory.org/stellar-quotes.html.

Historic Food. "Possets." Accessed April 28, 2015. http://www.historicfood.com/Posset%20Recipes.htm.

Joelle's Sacred Grove. "Pagan Hymns, Carols, and other Assorted Songs." Accessed April 28, 2015. http://www.joellessacredgrove.com/Carols/carols.html.

MacCulloch, J. A. "The Cult of the Dead" in *The Religion of the Ancient Celts*. Sacred Texts. Last modified 2011. http://www.sacred-texts.com/neu/celt/rac/rac13.htm.

McMorrow-Hernandez, Joshua. "7 Tips or Tricks to Make It Snow." Accessed April 27, 2015. http://weather.thefuntimesguide.com/2010/01/make_it_snow.php.

Miles, Clement A. "The Christmas-Tree, Decorations, and Gifts." *Christmas in Ritual and Tradiation*, 1912. Sacred Texts. http://www.sacred-texts.com/time/crt/crt15.htm.

National Christmas Tree Association. Last revised 2013. http://www.realchristmastrees.org/dnn/default.aspx.

The Order of Bards, Ovates, and Druids. "The Mistletoe Foundation." Accessed April 27, 2015. http://www.druidry.org/library/library/mistletoe-foundation.

Pearse, Roger. "The Roman Cult of Mithras." The Tertullian Project. Last modified May 24, 2014. http://www.tertullian.org/rpearse/mithras/display.php?page=main.

Rampant Scotland. "New Year's Eve—Hogmanay." Accessed April 27, 2015. http://www.rampantscotland.com/know/blknow12.htm.

Roberts, Rachel. "Top Rituals to Make It Snow." Last revised March 14, 2012. http://blog.skiheavenly.com/2012/03/14/top-rituals-to-make-it-snow/.

Shaw, George Bernard. "Inspirational Quotes." Accessed April 28, 2015. http://thinkexist.com/quotation/better_keep_yourself_clean_and_bright-you_are_the/147711.html.

Smith, Michael. "How to get a Snow Day in Four Easy Steps." Last revised January 11, 2011. http://www.principalspage.com/theblog/archives/how-to-get-a-snow-day-in-4-easy-steps.

Sparber, Max. "Tomte: Scandinavian Christmas traditions at the American Swedish Institute. Last modified December 6, 2011. http://tinyurl.com/m6da2k5.

St. Nicholas Center. "Who is Saint Nicholas?" Last modified 2015. http://www.stnicholascenter.org/pages/who-is-st-nicholas/.

Swanton, John. R. "Tlingit Myths and Texts." Bureau of American Ethnology Bulletin 39 (1909). Accessed April 28, 2015. http://sacred-texts.com/nam/nw/tmt/index.htm.

Willow, Vibra. "Wheel of the Year." Reclaiming. Last modified 2000. http://www.reclaiming.org/about/witchfaq/wheelofyear.html.

Wodening, Swain. "Yuletide Rituals and Sedes." Frigga's Web. Last modified September 17, 2012. http://www.friggas-web.org/yuletide.html.

Woodruff, Betsy. "Forget Santa. You should celebrate La Befana." Last modified December 22, 2014. http://tinyurl.com/nu5xerb.

INDEX

mummering, 29, 31, 32, 47, 54, 166, 202, 204

N

New Year, 7, 24, 26, 28, 29, 32-34, 36-39, 46, 47, 81, 99-101, 140, 205, 208

O

Omen Days, 100

P

Pagans, 1, 2, 8-10, 16, 19, 23, 24, 28, 32, 43-45, 47, 55, 64, 67-70, 73, 81, 92, 105, 134, 146, 158, 163, 167, 168, 186, 194

petitions, 35, 36, 75, 81, 163, 186, 189

plants, 5, 7, 30, 35, 44, 49, 51, 60, 76, 79, 82, 85, 87, 90, 99, 127, 132, 140, 167, 197-200

Porta-Pagan magick set craft, 92

protective lorica for Yule, 81-82

protection, 6, 36, 49, 53, 77, 81, 82, 86, 87, 92, 132, 133, 135, 179, 181, 198-200